IELTS Masterclass

Teacher's Book

Andrew Jurascheck

OXFORD
UNIVERSITY PRESS

D0814314

OXFORD
UNIVERSITY PRESS

Great Clarendon Street, Oxford OX2 6DP

Oxford University Press is a department of the University of Oxford.
It furthers the University's objective of excellence in research, scholarship,
and education by publishing worldwide in

Oxford New York

Auckland Cape Town Dar es Salaam Hong Kong Karachi
Kuala Lumpur Madrid Melbourne Mexico City Nairobi
New Delhi Shanghai Taipei Toronto

With offices in

Argentina Austria Brazil Chile Czech Republic France Greece
Guatemala Hungary Italy Japan Poland Portugal Singapore
South Korea Switzerland Thailand Turkey Ukraine Vietnam

OXFORD and OXFORD ENGLISH are registered trade marks of
Oxford University Press in the UK and in certain other countries

ISBN: 978 0 19 457535 5

Printed in China

Contents

Student's Book Contents   4

Introduction   6

1   Cultural differences   11

2   Conflicting interests   19

3   Fitness and health   27

4   The arts   34

5   Work and business   41

6   Education   48

7   Science   55

8   IT and communications   62

9   Social issues   69

10 The natural world   76

11 Psychology   83

12 Engineering and innovation   90

13 History and archaeology   97

14 Language   102

Student's Book Contents

Unit and Theme	Reading	Listening	Speaking
1 Cultural differences pages 9–20	*The pursuit of happiness* Skills: reading for gist, unfamiliar vocabulary IELTS practice: short-answer questions, sentence and summary completion	*Applying to study abroad* Section 1 IELTS practice: note and form completion	*Meeting people* Skills: describing your origins IELTS practice: Part 1 familiar discussion
2 Conflicting interests pages 21–32	*The other population crisis* Skills: paragraph summaries IELTS practice: matching headings	*Congestion charging scheme* Section 2 IELTS practice: note and sentence completion	*Changing places* Skills: speaking from notes IELTS practice: Part 2 extended speaking
3 Fitness and health pages 33–44	*The power of nothing* Skills: text structure, finding evidence IELTS practice: Yes/No/Not given, True/False/Not given	*University sports centre* Section 3 IELTS practice: matching lists, classification	*What do you really know about food?* Skills: giving reasons IELTS practice: Part 3 topic discussion
4 The arts pages 45–56	*When is a room not a room?* Skills: style, text structure, using question stems IELTS practice: multiple-choice questions, short-answer questions, global multiple-choice	*Musical instruments* Section 4 IELTS practice: labelling a diagram, note completion	*Arts events* Skills: getting started IELTS practice: Part 2 extended speaking
5 Work and business pages 57–68	*The great work myth* Skills: reading for gist, key words IELTS practice: sentence completion, summary completion	*Job enquiry* Section 1 IELTS practice: multiple-choice questions, labelling a map	*Jobs* Skills: describing an occupation IELTS practice: Part 1 familiar discussion
6 Education pages 69–80	*The education gender gap* Skills: scanning, identifying opinions IELTS practice: matching, sentence completion	*University clubs and societies* Section 2 IELTS practice: short-answer questions, sentence completion	*Learning styles* Skills: personal reactions IELTS practice: Part 2 extended speaking
7 Science pages 81–92	*Stars in their eyes* Skills: description schemes, reading for gist IELTS practice: labelling a diagram, multiple-answer questions, True/False/Not given	*Ethics in science* Section 3 IELTS practice: multiple-choice questions, multiple-answer questions	*Moral dilemmas* Skills: advantages and disadvantages IELTS practice: Part 3 topic discussion

Language for writing	Writing	Help yourself	Unit and Theme
Describing data Similarities	*Cultural data* Skills: accurate description, selecting main features IELTS practice: task 1	How to use the *Help yourself* pages	**1 Cultural differences** pages 9–20
Consecutive noun phrases Avoiding repetition	*Environment issues* Skills: taking a view and developing it IELTS practice: task 2	Global issues	**2 Conflicting interests** pages 21–32
Relative clauses	*Health issues* Skills: organizing ideas, using organizing expressions IELTS practice: task 2	Vocabulary	**3 Fitness and health** pages 33–44
Choosing tenses	*Spending on the arts* Skills: describing trends, describing figures IELTS practice: task 1	Reading more widely	**4 The arts** pages 45–56
Comparative and superlative forms	*Advertising* Skills: comparing data IELTS practice: task 1	Word formation	**5 Work and business** pages 57–68
-ing forms and infinitives	*Student finance* Skills: introductions IELTS practice: task 2	Thinking skills	**6 Education** pages 69–80
Passive forms	*Scientific processes* Skills: sequencing IELTS practice: task 1	English spelling	**7 Science** pages 81–92

Unit and Theme	Reading	Listening	Speaking
IT and communications 8 pages 93–104	*Technology text* Skills: making notes IELTS practice: table completion, multiple-choice question	*Wikipedia* Section 4 IELTS practice: short-answer questions, flow chart and summary completion	*Future technology* Skills: speculating about the future IELTS practice: Part 3 topic discussion
Social issues 9 pages 105–116	*The invisible thread* Skills: word formation IELTS practice: locating information, Yes/No/Not given	*Volunteering* Section 1 IELTS practice: note completion, short-answer questions	*Cultural identity* Skills: giving a presentation IELTS practice: Part 2 extended speaking
The natural world 10 pages 117–128	*Armed and dangerous* Skills: paragraph summaries, unfamiliar vocabulary IELTS practice: matching headings, sentence completion, short-answer questions	*Nature reserves* Section 2 IELTS practice: note completion, multiple-answer questions	*Zoos* Skills: expressing opinions IELTS practice: Part 3 topic discussion
Psychology 11 pages 129–140	*The phantom hand* Skills: finding specific information, text organization IELTS practice: classifying statements, multiple-choice questions, summary completion	*Personality testing* Section 4 IELTS practice: sentence completion, multiple-choice questions, short-answer questions	*Free-time activities* Skills: describing interests IELTS practice: Part 1 familiar discussion
Engineering and innovation 12 pages 141–152	*Tower of strength* Skills: text organization IELTS practice: classification, locating information, short-answer questions	*Survival watch* Section 4 IELTS practice: short-answer questions, labelling a diagram	*Design* Skills: describing objects IELTS practice: Part 2 extended speaking
History and archaeology 13 pages 153–164	*The lost civilization of Peru* Skills: text organization IELTS practice: True/False/Not given, note completion, multiple-answer question	*Ashmolean Museum* Section 2 IELTS practice: note and table completion	*Past and present* Skills: changes over time IELTS practice: Part 3 topic discussion
Language 14 pages 165–176	*Hyperpolyglots* Skills: scanning IELTS practice: matching list, summary completion, multiple-answer question	*Mother language* Section 4 IELTS practice: sentence completion, multiple-answer questions, multiple-choice questions	*Reading habits* IELTS practice: full speaking test

Language for writing	Writing	Help yourself	Unit and Theme
Adverbs and adverbial phrases	*Effects of technology* Skills: supporting ideas IELTS practice: task 2	Using the Internet	**IT and communications** pages 93–104
Collocation	*Individuals and the state* Skills: academic style IELTS practice: task 2	Giving presentations	**Social issues** pages 105–116
Concession	*Animal populations* Skills: organizing information IELTS practice: task 1	Easily confused words	**The natural world** pages 117–128
Articles	*What motivates people* Skills: common errors, punctuation IELTS practice: task 2	Planning remedial work	**Psychology** pages 129–140
Expressing purpose Cause and effect	*Aviation* Skills: organizing a description IELTS practice: task 1	Subject-specific vocabulary	**Engineering and innovation** pages 141–152
Conditionals	*Museums* Skills: argument and hypothesis IELTS practice: task 2	Pronunciation: individual sounds	**History and archaeology** pages 153–164
Sentence focus Placing emphasis	*Language* Skills: revision of planning IELTS practice: task 2	Pronunciation: word stress	**Language** pages 165–176

A guide to the IELTS modules

IELTS is divided into four modules, taken in the order below.

Listening
(30 minutes)

In each section you will hear a recording. The four sections become progressively more difficult and each recording is played once only. There are pauses to divide the recording into smaller parts. For each part you need to answer a series of questions of one type. References to examples of each question type are given in the table.

Section	Number of items	Text type	Task types
1	10	social or transactional conversation (2 speakers)	completing notes, table, sentences, diagram, flow chart or summary (page 15)
2	10	talk or speech on social needs (1 speaker)	short-answer questions (page 75)
3	10	conversation in educational context (2–4 speakers)	various kinds of multiple-choice questions (page 62)
4	10	talk or lecture on topic of general interest (1 speaker)	labelling parts of a diagram (page 51)
			matching lists (page 39)
			sentence completion (page 27)

Academic Reading
(60 minutes)

The three passages contain 2000–2750 words in total and become progressively more difficult, but they are always suitable for non-specialist readers. If any technical terms are used, they will be explained in a glossary. References to examples of each question type are given in the table.

Passage	Number of items	Text type	Task types
1	11–15	topics of general interest	various kinds of multiple-choice questions (page 48)
2	11–15	non-specialist articles or extracts from books, journals, magazines and newspapers	short-answer questions (page 12)
3	11–15	one, at least, has detailed logical argument	sentence completion (page 12)
			classification (page 142)
			matching headings with paragraphs or sections of text (page 24)
			completing notes, sentences, tables, summary, diagram or flow chart (page 12)
			matching lists/phrases (page 72)
			locating information with paragraphs (page 144)
			true/false/not given (text information) (page 36)
			yes/no/not given (writer's views) (page 36)

Academic Writing
(60 minutes)

There is no choice of task, either in Part 1 or 2, so you must be prepared to write about any topic. However, the topics in the exam are of general interest and you do not need to be an expert to write about them. References to examples of each task type are given in the table.

Task	Time	Format	Task types
1	20 minutes	150-word report, describing or explaining a table or diagram (page 18)	presenting information based on: • data, e.g. bar charts, line graph, table • a process/procedure in various stages • an object, event or series of events
2	40 minutes	250-word essay, responding to written opinion/problem (page 30)	presenting and/or discussing: • your opinions • solutions to problems • evidence, opinions and implications • ideas or arguments

Speaking
(11–14 minutes)

You will be interviewed, on your own, by one Examiner, and the conversation will be recorded on audio cassette. The three-part structure of the interview is always the same, although the topics will vary from candidate to candidate. References to examples of each main part are given in the table.

Part	Time	Format	Task types
1	4–5 minutes	familiar discussion (page 16)	• Introduction, ID check • You answer questions about familiar topics: yourself, your home/family, job/studies, and interests.
2	3–4 minutes	extended speaking (page 28)	• You are given a topic verbally and on a card. You have a minute to prepare a talk. • You speak for 1–2 minutes on the topic, e.g. a person, place, object or event. • You answer one or two follow-up questions.
3	4–5 minutes	topic discussion (page 40)	• You answer verbal questions, discussing more abstract ideas linked to the topic of Part 2.

Twenty tips for IELTS success

1   In Listening, use the example at the beginning of the first section to familiarize yourself with the sound, the situation, and the speakers.

2   Keep listening until the recording stops, looking only at the questions that relate to the part being played.

3   There are often pauses in the recording between different sections. Use these to prepare for the next set of questions.

4   Answer Listening questions in the order they appear on the Question Paper. Remember that they normally follow the order of the information in the recording.

5   At the end of the recording you have some time to transfer your answers to the Answer Sheet. Check your grammar and spelling as you do so.

6   In Academic Reading, begin by going quickly through each passage to identify features such as the topic, the style, the likely source, the writer's purpose and the intended reader.

7   As you read, don't try to understand the precise meaning of every word or phrase. You don't have time, and those parts of the text might not be tested anyway.

8   Reading tasks sometimes have an example answer. If this is the case, study it and decide why it is correct.

9   Some tasks require you to use words from the text in the answer; in others you should use your own words. Check the instructions carefully.

10 The instructions may also include a word limit, e.g. Use no more than three words. Keep to this by avoiding unnecessary words in your answer.

11 In Academic Writing, you must always keep to the topic set. Never try to prepare sections of text before the exam.

12 Keep to the suggested timing: there are more marks possible for Task 2 than Task 1.

13 Organize and link your ideas and sentences appropriately, using a wide range of language and showing your ability (in Task 2) to discuss ideas and express opinions.

14 If you write less than 150 words in Task 1 or less than 250 in Task 2 you will lose marks, but there is no maximum number of words for either.

15 When you plan your essay, allow plenty of time at the end to check your work.

16 In Speaking, don't try to give a prepared speech, or talk about a different topic from the one you are asked to discuss.

17 Always speak directly to the Examiner, not to the recording equipment.

18 Whenever you reply 'Yes' or 'No' to the Examiner's questions, add more details to your answer. In each case, aim to explain at least one point.

19 Remember that you are not being tested on your general knowledge but on your ability to communicate effectively.

20 Organize and link your ideas and sentences appropriately, talking clearly at normal speed and using a wide range of structures and vocabulary.

1 Cultural differences

Introduction page 9

Issues – This section introduces the overall theme of the unit, introducing students to a range of different cultures and focusing on possible meanings of the term *culture*.

Aims – Students are given opportunities to hear and speak about a range of different global cultures, and to consider and discuss their own personal cultural contexts.

1 Ask students to work in pairs or groups to discuss photos 1–4.

Key

a Photo 1 shows a young Sherpa living in the mountains of Nepal.
Photo 2 shows a villager in the Alaskan island of Shishmaref.
Photo 3 shows a Quechua Indian living in the Peruvian Andes.
Photo 4 shows the Sami people of Scandinavia.

b All the people live in small communities away from modern cities. The environment in each photo is difficult in its own way.
Photo 1: The clothing worn by the boy in the photo suggests a fairly traditional culture in a climate which might be cool even when the sun is shining. The background indicates that this is one of the mountainous regions of the world.
Photo 2: The clothing worn by the person in the photo, and the snow and ice visible in the background, show that this is a very cold climate. Their activity and lifestyle is probably limited by the climate.
Photo 3: The high mountains indicate that this is probably somewhere in the Andes. The clothes the person in the photo is wearing suggests a traditional way of life. She is high in the mountains, but there are ruins of a town in the background. It seems to be a remote area, but there may be tourism.
Photo 4: The clothing worn by the people in the photo and other items visible suggest a fairly simple, traditional culture in a cold climate. The people are cooking fish which may mean that they find their own food rather than buy it.

2 Students decide the answers individually based on their own general knowledge before discussing them in pairs.

Key

1 C (beef)
2 B (no running water)
3 C (llamas)
4 B (reindeer round-up)

Recording script

Narrator: The people in the photographs live on different continents. How much can you guess about their lives? Photograph 1 shows people living in the mountains of Nepal. If you lived here, what would you be unlikely to eat for dinner? Would it be, A: anchar, a kind of spicy pickle, B: cheese, C: beef, or D: salad?
OK. Now, photograph 2 shows a villager from the Alaskan island of Shishmaref. What modern convenience would be unavailable if you lived here? Would it be, A: electricity, B: running water, C: the telephone, or D: television?
In photograph 3 you can see a Quechua Indian from the Peruvian Andes. If you lived here, which of these animals would you be likely to tend for a living? Would it be, A: goats, B: cows C: llamas, or D: chickens?
Finally, photograph 4 shows the Sami people in the North of Scandinavia. A popular game is played with animal hoof bones. What do you think it's called? Is it A: the bone game, B: reindeer roundup C: throwing bones, or D: wishbone pull?

3 Recording script

Narrator: So, let's see how well you did. Here are the answers to the four questions. The answer to Question 1 is **C, beef**. In Nepal the cow is considered a sacred animal and legally protected from slaughter.

Question 2. The answer is **B. Most people in Shishmaref do not have running water in their houses. They collect rain or gather ice blocks to melt for drinking water.**
Question 3. The answer to this question is **C, llamas.** The Quechua people of the Andes depend on the llama because it can carry loads at any altitude while providing people with wool, leather, meat and dung fuel.
Question 4. The answer to the last question is **B. The bones are used to represent the people herding their animals and the reindeer on which their livelihood depends.**

4 Possible answers

c Students might list some of the following: customs associated with work, marriage, festivals, food and drink, clothing, treatment and behaviour of children; beliefs associated with animals, religion, members of other communities, behaviour towards different members of society.

Reading page 10

Issues – This section introduces the idea of a measurable scale of happiness and how the level of happiness varies in different parts of the world.
Aims – Students learn how to read for gist and gain a general understanding of a written text without needing to understand all of the vocabulary.

Orientation

1 Key

a It shows broad levels of happiness in different countries. Countries are arranged in order from happiest to least happy.
b Nigeria has the highest percentage of very happy people. Between 65 and 70% of the population are very happy.
Romania has the lowest percentage of very happy people. Less than 5% of the population are very happy.
The USA has a lower percentage of very happy people than Mexico. The chart shows a figure of about 60% for Mexico and about 40% for the USA.
Australia has a much higher percentage of very happy people than Russia. Over 40% of Australians are very happy, compared with less than 10% of Russians.

2 Ask students to work in groups to discuss the questions and then report back to the class.

Possible answers

a Culture: The way of life can vary enormously from one country to another. In some countries people feel a pressure to succeed and tend to work under a lot of stress; in others the pace of life is slower and there is a greater emphasis placed on things like family, friends and relaxation.
Materialism: In many Western countries acquiring material possessions is given considerable importance, and so a great deal of effort is expended on wealth creation. In more traditional societies, money is of little or no significance, and material possessions are either not available or not particularly valued.
Basic needs: In some countries basic needs such as food, water and shelter are not by any means guaranteed. This can cause very significant levels of stress and unhappiness.
Climate: Most people require reasonable levels of daylight to sustain them, and many people are happier if they experience good levels of warmth and sunshine. In some countries there is very little daylight at certain times of year, and often little or no sunshine.

Reading for gist

3 Make sure that students read the Note. Tell them they should read the text through quickly the first time to understand the gist, rather than any specific details.

Key

the growth in the academic study of happiness
the distinction between happiness and overall 'satisfaction' with life
links between wealth, consumerism and happiness
cultural attitudes towards happiness

4 Key

the growth in the academic study of happiness (paragraphs 2 and 3)
the distinction between happiness and overall 'satisfaction' with life (paragraph 4)
links between wealth, consumerism and happiness (paragraphs 6 and 7)
cultural attitudes towards happiness (paragraphs 5 and 6)

Unfamiliar vocabulary

5 Make sure that students read the Note. Point out the importance of being able to understand the general meaning of a text even when some vocabulary is not understood. This is an important skill for tackling any reading text. Unfamiliar words might include the following: *downshifting, gurus, bona fide, risky*. Students should be able to understand the general meaning of these paragraphs without understanding these specific words.

IELTS practice

Questions 1–3: Short-answer questions

Key

1 where you live (line 6)
2 politicians (line 23)
3 money and inequality (line 31)

Questions 4–6: Sentence completion

Key

4 personal achievement (line 57)
5 inferior or guilty (line 64)
6 cultural standard (line 67)

Questions 7–10: Summary completion

Key

7 average incomes (line 76)
8 happiness suppressant (line 79)
9 young adults (line 80)
10 personal development (line 94)

Exploration

6 Students will have differing opinions, especially in a mixed nationality class. Encourage each group to discuss their differences, giving reasons for their opinions, before attempting to reach a concensus. Other factors could include: access to food, water and shelter; climate; amount of leisure time; access to nature; the pace of life, etc.

7 Key

satisfied – dissatisfied
risky – safe
unwise – wise
precise – imprecise
meaningful – meaningless
collectivist – individualist
inferior – superior
significant – insignificant,
competitive – uncompetitive
miserable – happy

8 Key

a over-report = exaggerate; in this context it refers to people who say they are happier than they really are.
under-report = say things aren't as bad as they are; in this context to say they are not that happy.
Other verbs:
overbook, overcharge, overcook, overdo, overeat, overestimate, overload, overpay, over-react, oversimplify, overspend, overstate, overwork; undercharge, underestimate, underpay, underrate, understate, undervalue
b consumerism = the desire to acquire consumer goods and use services.
Other words ending in *-ism* grouped by meaning:
Political or religious belief:
socialism, conservatism, liberalism, feminism, Buddhism, Judaism, Sikhism, etc.
Attitudes and abstract qualities:
fanaticism, racism, sexism, cynicism, idealism
Creative artistic movements:
cubism, expressionism, impressionism, surrealism, post-modernism
c hard-headed = not allowing emotions to affect opinions and decisions.
hard-hearted = unkind or lacking in sympathy and feeling.
hard-pressed = experiencing difficulties, or under great pressure.
hard-nosed = tough, or not influenced by emotional considerations.

9 Key

to draw up league tables
to fulfil expectations (also fulfil someone's needs)
to gather data
to meet someone's needs (also meet expectations)
to suffer symptoms

10 Key

a gather data
b fulfil ... the expectations
c suffering ... symptoms
d draw up ... league tables
e meet ... needs

Listening page 14

Aims – Students learn how to do a form completion task and recognize the importance of predicting answer types.

Orientation

1 Ask students to work in pairs or groups to discuss questions a–d. Check that students know the meaning of *culture shock* (a feeling of confusion and anxiety that somebody may feel when they live in or visit another country).

Key

a Photo 1: Poland
   Photo 2: USA
   Photo 3: Hong Kong (China)
   Photo 4: The Dutch Island of Aruba in the South Caribbean, off Venezuela.

Possible answers

c To work: this could be a permanent move (economic migration), a temporary move to a particular job opportunity, or voluntary work (for example, aid work in a developing country). As a refugee: escaping war or persecution of some kind.
   To marry: if your partner is from a different country.
   For a change of climate or lifestyle: for example, many people move to the Mediterranean because the climate is very pleasant.

Predicting answer types

2 Make sure that students read the Note. Encourage them to guess possible answers based on the information contained in the form. Check that students know the meaning of semester (one of the two periods that the school or college year is divided into, used especially in American English). The more common British English word *term* is usually used to describe one of three periods that a year is divided into.

Possible answers

a educational / about university courses / factual information
b 2 (a number between 1 and 9)
   3 (a number)
   5 (a date)
c 1 (a noun)
   4 (a noun)
   6 (a noun)

IELTS practice

Questions 1–6: Note completion

Key

1 a first degree
2 7
3 ten hours
4 second semester
5 27
6 international organizations

Recording script

Questions 1–6

Adviser:	Hello, Admissions Guidance, how can I help?
Student:	Hello, I'd like some information about studying at your university. Can you help me?
Adviser:	Yes, of course. What course are you interested in applying for?
Student:	International Business. I already have a first degree from a university in my country.
Adviser:	Fine, so you'd want to do a Master's level course?
Student:	Yes, that's right.
Adviser:	OK, we offer an MIB course – that's a twelve-month full-time course. I can send you details of that course or you can download a pdf file from our website.
Student:	Could you put it in the post, please – I don't have access to the Internet at the moment. Could you tell me what qualifications I need for that course?
Adviser:	Yes, for the MIB, you need **a first degree**. The minimum qualification is a 'two one' or a 'first'.
Student:	OK.
Adviser:	And in English language you need a score of 7 or above in IELTS.
Student:	That's not a problem. I have a 9.
Adviser:	That's fine.
Student:	Could you tell me the course hours and the semester dates, please?
Adviser:	Yes, there's a total of **ten hours** of lectures, seminars, and tutorials a week, and there's an **extended stay abroad** at the beginning of the **second semester**. That involves spending a month at the national head office of a multinational corporation.
Student:	OK.
Adviser:	And the semester dates are, just a moment, OK – the first semester starts on twenty-seventh of September and ends on the twenty-second of January, and the second semester runs from the seventh of February to the the **twenty-seventh of May**.

Student:	Can you tell me a bit more about the actual course content?
Adviser:	Well, I don't know much about the course personally – I'm an admissions officer, but I can read the course description for you if you like. If you need to know more about the academic side, you'll need to speak to the course tutor.
Student:	Thanks – I'd be very grateful if you could tell me as much as possible now.
Adviser:	I'll just read the main points: 'it involves the advanced study of **international organizations**, their management and their changing external context. Students develop their ability to apply knowledge and understanding of international business to complex issues, both systematically and creatively, to improve business practice.'
Student:	Thank you very much.
Adviser:	You're welcome. Now, if you could give me your name and address, I'll have full details of postgraduate courses sent to you.
Student:	OK, my name is Javed Iqbal ...

Questions 7–10: Form completion

Key

7	5	9	First
8	Economics	10	Urdu and English

Recording script

Questions 7–10

Student:	OK, my name is Javed Iqbal. That's J- A- V- E- D ... I- Q- B- A- L.
Adviser:	Thank you. And your home address Mr Iqbal?
Student:	It's Aga Khan Road, Shalimar **5**, Islamabad, Pakistan.
Adviser:	Thank you, and could I ask you one or two more questions for our records?
Student:	Yes, of course.
Adviser:	What was your first degree in?
Student:	I did **Economics**. I got a **first** class degree.
Adviser:	And where did you study?
Student:	At the university here in Islamabad.
Adviser:	OK. Now, you said you had an IELTS level 9. Could I ask what your first language is?
Student:	Actually, I'm bilingual in **Urdu and English**.
Adviser:	Thank you very much. I'll put full details in the post today.

Student:	Thank you – and thanks for all the information.
Adviser:	Not at all, Mr Iqbal. Thank you for calling.

Exploration

3 These questions are intended to encourage students to explore the wider aspects of the topic, drawing on their own experience where possible.

Speaking page 16

Issues – This section introduces the theme of first meetings.

Aims – Students practise discussing familiar, everyday topics as required in Speaking Part 1.

Orientation

1 Ask students to work in pairs to discuss questions a–c. In mixed nationality classes, ask students of the same nationality to work together if possible, before comparing answers with the whole class.

Possible answers

b Mutual friends: we often begin a conversation by finding out whether the other person knows anybody we know.
What they do: one of the first questions many people ask is '*What (job) do you do?*'
Where they live: depending on circumstances, the country; or perhaps details about the town or even the street.
Their family: how many people in the family, where the family comes from, perhaps even what the other members of the family do.
Likes and dislikes: after the initial introductions, the next things to discuss may well be favourite music, food, hobbies, etc.

c These vary greatly in different cultures. However, some taboos are common to many cultures, for example, death, explicit discussion of sex, talking about income, criticising close family and friends, and so on.

Describing your origins

2 Key

Speaker 1: e	Speaker 4: d
Speaker 2: c	Speaker 5: a
Speaker 3: b	

Recording script

Speaker 1: **My home town** is a medium-sized market town. It's about a hundred kilometres from the capital city. It's on a river and quite near the mountains. About ten thousand people live there. A lot of people from the town work in a sugar factory.

Speaker 2: **What I really like most about my village is** the people. They're so friendly. Everyone knows everyone else and that makes you feel very safe and comfortable.

Speaker 3: **The main thing I dislike is** the traffic – it's getting worse every year. It's almost impossible to cross the road in the town centre during the day. And the parking is terrible. There aren't enough car parks and people park all over the place.

Speaker 4: **I think they'd find** its old buildings **very interesting**. There's an ancient church with beautiful paintings on the walls inside. Visitors come from quite long distances to see those. Also the town hall is very impressive – it's over four hundred years old and they still use it everyday.

Speaker 5: **The main improvement would be** more sports and entertainment facilities. There's not much for young people to do, which means they have to catch the train to the nearest town if they want a good night out. We've got an old cinema and a couple of football pitches at the moment – that's all.

3 Key

Speaker 1: My home town is ...
Speaker 2: What I really like most about my village is ...
Speaker 3: The main thing I dislike is ...
Speaker 4: I think they'd find ... very interesting
Speaker 5: The main improvement would be ...

4 Encourage students to give full answers, as in the recordings.

Everyday questions

5 Possible answers

Can you tell me something about your family / friends / country?
What's your favourite (type of) food / holiday?
What do you (most) like / dislike about learning English / your country / travelling abroad?
What sort of things do you do in your spare time / on holiday?

IELTS practice
Part 1: Familiar discussion

This exercise is intended to introduce and practise the type of questions students will face in Speaking Part 1. Make sure students read the Note. Remind them again to give full answers, and check that they are responding appropriately to the questions asked.

Language for writing page 17

Aims – Students learn to interpret data in graph form, and practise the language of similarities which they will need to use in Writing Task 1.

Describing data

1 Key

a Chart A shows the regions of the world where students in the class are from.
b Each section represents the numbers of students from the different areas.
c The composition changed so that by 2005 there were considerably more women than men.
d There were more or less equal numbers of male and female students in 2002 and 2003
e Taken together the figures indicate that more students are passing exams.
f From graph C we can draw the conclusion that the trend for men and women is similar. Women do consistently better than men.

2 Tell students to read through the ideas in the Student's Book. Then brainstorm alternative ideas and make a list on the board. Students choose the subject that interests them most. Allow 5 to 10 minutes for each student to obtain information from all the other members of the class.

Similarities

4 This exercise introduces students to some of the basic language of similarities which will be useful for describing data in Writing Task 1.
Ask students to discuss questions a–e in pairs before comparing answers as a full class.

Key

a Incorrect: Canada has French as a main language.
b Incorrect: Spanish is spoken in most South American countries, but Portuguese is spoken in Brazil, Dutch in Surinam, English in Guyana, and French in French Guiana.
c Correct.
d Correct.

e Incorrect: Britain is one of the few EC countries where the euro has not replaced the original currency (the pound). There are only a few shops where euros are accepted.

5 Key

a **Neither** Canada **nor** Australia
b **all** the countries
c In **each** country
d **Both** Mexico **and** Norway
e **either** pounds **or** euros

6 With a monolingual class choose task b. Mixed nationality classes can choose either task a or task b.

Writing page 18

Aims – Students learn the importance of using a clear introduction when summarizing data, and learn to be selective about the information they include.

Accurate description

1 Key

a 1 transport
  2 housework
  3 household size
  4 participation in sport or physical activity
b 1 between different modes of transport: train, bus, car
  2 difference between time spent on household tasks by men and women of varying ages
  3 relative numbers of households of different sizes from 1 person to six or more
  4 participation in sport or physical activity by people of varying ages
c Totals: 1 (vertical axis marked with billions of passenger kilometres)
  Proportions: 3 (a pie chart like this shows the proportion of the total for each group illustrated)
  Percentages: 4 (vertical axis marked with percentages)
  Averages: 2 and 4 (figures in these charts show averages for each age group listed, because an age range is given in each case)
d 1 1952–2002
  2 2000–2001
  3 2003
  4 2000–2001

2 Key

The statement relates to illustration 2. Information included: *the average number of hours per day* = the unit of measurement on the vertical axis of the illustration; *on household tasks* = what the measurement relates to; *males and females of different age groups* = the groupings used on the horizontal axis; *in the UK* = the place referred to

Point out that words like *show* and *represent* from Student's Book page 17 (exercise 3) are useful in accurate descriptions.

3 Make sure that students read the Note and point out that this is the best way to introduce a Writing Task 1 that involves describing data.

Possible answers

1 The graph shows the total number of kilometres per year travelled in Britain by three modes of transport – train, bus and car – during the period 1952–2002.
3 The chart indicates the proportion of UK households consisting of differing numbers of people from one to six or more in 2003.
4 The chart shows the average number of UK citizens of different age groups who participated in sport or physical activity in the period 2000–2001.

4 Possible answers

The home: That men are not expected to share the housework with women 50:50.
The family: that living alone rather than with the family is normal and acceptable. That large families are not very common.
Transport: people travel more than they used to. They travel many more miles by car.
Leisure: younger people spend much more time on physical activities than older people.

Selecting main features

5 Possible answers

The precise order could vary, but sentences F and E provide the best general summary of the information in the chart, while sentences B and A focus on main details. Sentences C and G deal with minor details which are irrelevant to the main features of the illustration. The information in sentence D repeats the information from sentence F in a less useful form, while sentence H is an opinion and not based on information given in the chart.
1 F 2 E 3 B 4 A 5 C 6 G 7 D 8 H

6 If students have difficulty with this, explain that a description should concentrate on summarizing the information and highlighting the main details. Minor details and opinions do not need to be included.

Key

Include: F, E, B, A
Omit: C, G, D, H

7 Make sure that students read the Note. Point out the importance of focusing on significant detail and ignoring minor points or irrelevant detail.

Possible answers

1 During the period 1952–2002 there was a steep increase in the number of miles travelled by people in cars. During the same period, the number of miles travelled by bus declined slightly and train travel remained roughly the same.

3 Approximately two-thirds of the population live in one- or two-person households. Roughly a quarter of people live in three- and four-person households.

4 Participation in sport and other physical activities decreases steadily as age increases. Almost four times as many people in the 8–15 age group participate in sport and physical activity compared with those aged 65 and over.

Think, plan, write

8 Key

a 1 The number of visits by both UK residents and overseas residents overall rose steadily between 1982 and 2002.

2 The average length of stay by both UK residents and overseas residents fell slightly over the period 1982–2002.

Suggested answers

b For graph 1 include the information that the overall number of visits rose for both groups and that the rate of increase was greater for UK residents than for overseas residents. Omit any reference to slight fluctuations in the rate of increase or any opinions as to the reason for these figures.

For graph 2 include the information that the average length of stay fell for both UK residents and overseas visitors; that the percentage decrease was greater for the visits made by overseas residents than UK residents; and that UK residents made longer visits than overseas residents. Omit any reference to slight fluctuations in the average rate of decrease or any opinions as to the reason for these figures. Connect the information between the two graphs by including this comparison: visits to and from the UK became more frequent, but they tended to be shorter in duration.

c Similarities: The figures for UK residents are higher than those for overseas residents in both. Differences: Graph 1 shows a steady increase, graph 2 shows a steady decrease. In graph 1 the figure for UK residents is increasing more rapidly than that for overseas residents, whereas in graph 2 the figures for overseas residents are decreasing slightly more rapidly than those for UK residents.

Help yourself page 20

The final page in each unit is intended to include a variety of extra areas that students can explore and to encourage responsibility for their own language learning.

How to use the Help yourself pages

1 This exercise is intended to raise students' awareness of different possible approaches to studying. There are no right answers.

3 Key

solve your own problems in English: Units 3, 5, 11
improve how clearly you speak: Units 9, 13, 14
make fewer mistakes in writing: Units 7, 10, 12
develop your own ideas: Units 2, 6
get information to support your study: Units 2, 4, 8

IELTS to do list

Encourage the students to tick one of the boxes and plan to do this task outside class.

Where to look

Students can use these practical tips to find further information.

2 Conflicting interests

Introduction page 21

Issues – This section introduces the overall theme of the unit, focusing on a variety of environmental issues which give rise to conflicting interests.

Aims – Students are given opportunities to hear and speak about a range of different issues and to relate these to their own background.

1 Ask students to work in pairs or groups to discuss photos 1–3.

Possible answers

a Photo 1 shows the problem of waste disposal.
Photo 2 shows the problem of noise pollution and aviation fuel.
Photo 3 shows the problem of deforestation.

2 Check that students know the meaning of *split* (divided into two or more groups) and *hazardous* (highly dangerous).

Possible answer

Those in favour of the plans believe that this may provide good business for a local company and plenty of jobs. Those against the plans object to the health and safety risks, and the potential damage to the environment involved in this kind of work.

3 Key

a 1 environmentalists from *Green Earth*
2 the director of a local employment agency
3 the manager of the company who will do the work
4 a local resident and town councillor
b 1 against the plans
2 for the plans
3 for the plans
4 against the plan

Recording script

Presenter:	Next up on Northeast news, a story which involves complex issues and conflicting interests. The decision about whether or not to allow the dismantling of hazardous ships to go ahead in the area will not be an easy one for the authorities to reach. We'll start by hearing from the organization *Green Earth*, which has strong views on the subject.
Speaker 1:	As environmentalists, we are very concerned about the environmental and health risk posed by the breaking up of these ghost ships in Britain. The vessels are carrying a number of highly toxic substances including oil and asbestos. It's been reported that more than half the ships are already leaking or have a high risk of leaking in the future.
Presenter:	The director of a local employment agency has equally strong views.
Speaker 2:	I'm fed up of all this negative publicity, like the views we've just heard. We really ought to be celebrating the fact that one of our region's companies has got the world-class recycling facilities necessary to undertake this important work. In the past most contracts of this kind have gone to companies in the Far East.
Presenter:	A manager of the company which won the contract in the face of stiff international competition points out that what is good for his company and its shareholders is also good for the town.
Speaker 3:	This contract, the first of many we hope, will create two hundred permanent jobs in the town. That's 200 new jobs that will breathe life back into our dying industry. We've got the experience and we've got the expertise. We should seize the opportunity with both hands and bring an injection of much-needed cash into the town.
Presenter:	We'll finish with the perhaps more

balanced views of a local resident, who is incidentally also a town councillor.

Speaker 4: I've lived in this town all my life and I detest the scourge of unemployment we've had to live with for the last thirty years. We desperately need these jobs, everyone knows we do, but not at any cost. In the end the safety of our workers and our environment must be our priority. In the end, we need to think of future generations, not just ourselves.

4 Ask students to work in pairs or groups to discuss these questions.

Possible answers

a Cutting down rainforests. Economic arguments: This would create more agricultural land for growing populations and enable timber to be sold for profit. Environmental arguments: It would destroy habitats and add to global warming.
A hydro-electric scheme which requires areas of land to be flooded. Economic arguments: This would generate electricity and create jobs in the construction and maintenance of the plant. Environmental arguments: It would destroy habitats and force people to move.
The siting of nuclear power stations. Economic arguments: These would generate power, create jobs in the construction and maintenance of the plant. Environmental arguments: There are dangers of nuclear radiation through leaks or accidents, and problems invloved in decommissioning (closing down) the plant safely.

b These conflicts are occurring more frequently because of the growing world population and increasing industrialization which put pressure on natural resources.

Reading page 22

Issues – This section introduces the topic of population change and its possible future impact on the planet.

Aims – Students learn to summarize the main points of the paragraphs of a text and apply this to answering IELTS matching heading questions.

Orientation

1 Possible answer

The first photo shows a large extended family in which several generations are present. The second photo shows a small nuclear family with one child.
Larger families contribute to an increase in

population, causing a possible strain on resources (food, land, water, etc). However, larger families may provide their own support network by looking after younger and older members. Where smaller nuclear families are the norm, the burden of care is more likely to fall on the state. In small families, children may get more individual attention, but they have fewer family relationships and may have a higher burden of expectation on them.

2 Key

1 b   2 a   3 a   4 c

Paragraph summaries

4 Exercises 4 and 5 are intended to illustrate the importance of being able to understand and pick out the main point of each paragraph of a text. This also prepares students for the IELTS matching headings task.

Possible answers

a The world's population is growing at an alarming rate which is leading inevitably to future disaster.
b Continued world population growth is not inevitable and world population will peak at some point in the future and then decline.

5 Make sure that students are only writing one sentence summaries for each paragraph.

Possible answers

Paragraph C People are having fewer children.
Paragraph D European families choose to have one or two children, mainly for economic reasons.
Paragraph E There are a variety of reasons for declining populations in other countries.
Paragraph F The major impact of falling populations is that it will be difficult to support the growing proportion of older people.
Paragraph G The negative impact on the human population will be counter-balanced by a positive effect on the planet.

6 Possible answer

a Paragraph A includes a description of the future of the planet, opening with the phrase, *It is an unquestioned principle …*

Key

b Paragraph B vii *Now, it seems, population analysts have suddenly started to question the 'self-evident' truth that we are destined eventually to drown under our own weight.* (lines 10-13)

IELTS practice
Questions 1–5: Matching headings

Make sure that students read the Note and remind them to refer to their own summaries when choosing headings from the list. Check that students know the meaning of *fluctuating* (going up and down).

Key

1 Paragraph C: iii ... *people are having fewer and fewer children* (lines 20–21)
2 Paragraph D: vi ... *couples will have only or two children when they might have had three or four in the past* (line 38–40)
3 Paragraph E: ix *The causes of declining numbers in other countries are more varied and more alarming* (lines 53–54).
4 Paragraph F: viii *There will be no workforce if people do not have children.* (lines 81–82); *More and more old people will have to be supported by fewer and fewer young people* (lines 86–87).
5 Paragraph G: ii ... *mainstream economists are pessimistic. On the other hand, it is clear that reduced human numbers can only be good for the planet in the long term* (lines 95–98).

Exploration

7 Key

a Upward movement: rise (line 14), increase (line 26), soar (line 76), will have doubled (line 85–86), has grown (line l02)
Downward movement: Students can choose from decline (line 18), falling (line 25), go down (line 33), is dropping (line 54–55), go into steep decline (line 60–61), major drop (line 72), reduced (line 96)
b peak = to reach its highest point
c pool = available resource / stock of something
d *children* is the standard equivalent of *offspring*
e higher education = the stage of education beyond secondary state education; it includes college and university education. In many countries this starts at 18.
f Demographers study population levels and changes in birth and death rates.
g *ten thousand times* is the more informal way of saying *ten thousandfold*

8 Key

key questions	self-evident truth
patriotic duty	uncertain future
precious resources	vibrant economy

9 Key

a precious resources	d uncertain future
b self-evident truth	e vibrant economy
c patriotic duty	f key questions

10 Possible answer

b As the article suggests, population numbers may well start to decline. There is a growing awareness of the dangerous impact of human activities on the planet, and governments are beginning to take steps to control deforestation, pollution, global warming, and so on. On the other hand, it may be too late to avoid the worst effects of population increase: natural resources are running out, deforestation is still continuing at an alarming rate, and global warming is beginning to cause disruption to normal weather patterns. Most of the world's great wildernesses have already been extensively exploited by humans.

Listening page 26

Issues – this section introduces the topic of traffic congestion and looks at different ways of dealing with it.
Aims – Students learn how to tackle a note completion and sentence completion task and recognize the importance of studying the clues provided in the layout of exam questions.

Orientation

Ask students to work in pairs or groups to discuss questions a–d.

1 Key

a Photo 1 shows a very busy city scene with chaotic, slow-moving traffic. Photo 2 shows a city where there is much less traffic and it flows smoothly.
b In the first city, there are no measures in place to control traffic – such as traffic lanes, in particular lanes for buses – and the road system is very basic. In the second city, traffic control measures have been introduced and the road system is modern and well developed.
c It would be unpleasant to live in the first city, as journey times would be very long, parking would be difficult and pollution levels would be high. It would be much more pleasant to live in the second city, as moving around would be relatively easy.
d Cars with odd or even-numbered registration plates can only enter cities on designated days. This measure can be quite effective, although it is possible to get around it, for example by buying a second car with a different registration plate.
Making motorists pay charges for using certain areas at certain times. This measure can be effective, but unless there are good public transport alternatives motorists simply pay the charge and congestion is not significantly reduced.

Establishing priority lanes for buses, taxis, and bicycles. This measure is effective where the road system is sufficiently good to allow plenty of space for priority lanes and where the bus service is well funded. However, it needs to be effectively policed to ensure that motorists do not illegally use these lanes.

Encouraging car sharing and allowing cars with more than one person in them to use priority lanes. This measure can be effective, but people often like the independence of being able to chose when to travel and so it can be unpopular.

Investing heavily in public transport as an alternative to private cars. This is potentially the most effective measure, but by far the most expensive in the short term.

2 Possible answer

b Where is the area? How, when and where do you pay the charge? What happens if you don't pay? How is the system enforced? Do visitors from other countries have to pay the charge?

Information categories

3 Make sure that students read the Note and ask them to find the sub-headings in the panel for Questions 1–5 below.

Key

a Sub-headings:
When it applies
How much it costs
How to pay
b The notes also tell you what type of answers are needed in some cases: a time, a sum of money, etc.

IELTS practice
Questions 1–5: Note completion

Key

1 6.30 / half past six in the evening
2 £10
3 (automatic) penalty charge
4 text message
5 200

Recording script

Presenter: ... For more practical details, I'll pass you over to Jon Ward, from the London Tourist Agency.
Jon Ward: Thanks. So, that was a brief introduction to the congestion charging scheme, but if you're actually going to be driving your car in London on weekdays, there are a few more details you will need to know. Firstly, you don't need to worry about paying all the time. The charge applies between seven in the morning and **half past six** in the evening, Monday to Friday. You'll be pleased to hear however that, because the scheme is intended to reduce traffic during busy working hours, evenings and weekends are free. If you enter the zone during the charging times, you'll be eligible to pay the standard charge of eight pounds, which you can pay until ten o'clock on that day. After ten o'clock this charge rises to **ten pounds**. But be warned, if you fail to pay before midnight, you will have to pay an **automatic penalty charge**. In other words, there's no escape. Let's move on to paying. The charge, as I've said, is eight pounds a day, and the authorities have set up a number of systems to make it easy for you to pay, or rather to ensure that nobody has a good excuse for not paying. So, using your credit card, you can pay by phone, **by text message**, or on the Internet. The other option is to go to one of the **200** Pay Points inside the zone or the 9,500 Pay Points elsewhere in the country. If you know you're going to be driving in and out of London on a regular basis, you can buy weekly, monthly or annual passes, rather like a railway season ticket.

Questions 6–10: Sentence completion

Key

6 ring road
7 red background
8 registration plates
9 (the) underground
10 private vehicles

Recording script

Jon Ward: OK, on to the area itself. The congestion charging zone is everywhere inside London's inner **ring road**. For those of you not familiar with London's road system, this includes the City of London, that's the main financial district, and the West End, the commercial and entertainment centre. If you're still not sure, there are very clear signs on all roads which indicate when you are entering the area. These are round and have a white letter C on a **red background**. The scheme is policed by cameras which photograph all cars entering the area and send them to a computer which can recognize all

British and European car **registration plates**. If you pay the eight pound charge, you'll find London a little easier to drive round than it was before the charge was introduced. But if it's all too much trouble, and you decide to leave your car at home, then you are left with public transport: that's trains, buses, taxis or **the underground**. Some of the money from the congestion charging scheme is being used to upgrade public transport, so you should see improvements there. And because of reductions in the number of **private vehicles** on London's roads brought about by congestion charging, buses and taxis are providing a quicker, more efficient service than they did in the past. OK, I've covered the main details that you need to know.

Exploration

4 Possible answers

a Conflicting interests:
In favour: environmentalists who want to protect and improve the environment; commuters who feel their journeys would be made easier; businesses in the area who believe reduced traffic would make their businesses more accessible or more attractive places to work; residents living within the area.
Against: businesses who believe congestion charging would increase their costs and make their premises less accessible and a more inconvenient place to work; shops who rely on customers getting easy access; private individuals who prefer to go from door to door without paying additional charges.

b all emergency services; permanent residents; disabled drivers needing to access addresses in the area; taxis

Extra activity

On the board, write a list of the key opinion holders in the congestion charging issue: In favour – environmentalists, commuters, businesses, residents. Against – businesses, shops, private individuals. Divide the class into two: half the students take the role of a person who is in favour of the congestion charge and the other half a person who is against it. Give students three minutes to write down brief notes summarizing their opinions on the issue. Students work in pairs or groups of four to debate the issue.

Speaking page 28

Aims – Students practise speaking from notes as required in Speaking Part 2.

Speaking from notes

2 Make sure that students write notes, and not full sentences.

Possible answers

Photo 1
Location: in a derelict part of a city centre
Human activity: none visible
Atmosphere: very bleak, lonely
Photo 2
Location: on the side of a hill, in the countryside
Human activity: agricultural work
Atmosphere: peaceful, quiet

3 In pairs, tell students to choose one photo each. Tell them to imagine that they are familiar with this place. They should not use language of speculation, but describe it as if they know it well – if necessary they can add more details from their imagination.

IELTS practice
Part 2: Extended speaking

4 Tell students that they are going to practise a Speaking Part 2 task. Make sure that students read the Note and remind them to write about each point listed, using notes and not full sentences.

5 Students work in pairs. Ask them to time each other if possible and make a note of how long their partner spoke for.

Extra activity

Tell students to listen carefully to their partner's talk and note down a point which they want to hear more about. At the end of the talk they should ask a follow-up question on this point.

Language for writing page 29

Consecutive noun phrases

1 Key

a The purpose of the noun phrases is to provide more information, the first about a place (Hatfield Forest) and the second about an organization (The National Trust).

b Unlike relative clauses, these noun phrases do not include relative pronouns. However, like non-defining relative clauses, they are separated from the rest of the sentence by commas.

2 Key

a Stansted, London's third main airport, is in a largely agricultural area of Britain.

b Hatfield Forest, an ancient wooded area, is very close to Stansted Airport.

c Hatfield Forest, an area frequently visited by naturalists, is home to several thousand-year-old trees.

Avoiding repetition

3 Key

the former = aircraft
the latter = road traffic
such damage = damage caused by aircraft and road traffic
those = the expansion plans proposed recently
This area of woodland = Hatfield Forest
its = Hatfield Forest's
this atmosphere = the special tranquillity

4 Key

Hatfield Forest is a unique example of an ancient hunting forest. As a result, *it / the area / this area* has a rich but fragile natural structure. *This / This structure* will be damaged if noise and pollution increase. *The former* will drive away rare species of animals, and *the latter* will damage plant life. *This / Such damage* will be permanent.

Writing page 30

Orientation

1 Possible answers

a Agree: It is wrong to interfere with nature. Species have died out at varying rates throughout the history of the planet, and new species have always evolved to replace them.
Disagree: It is important to keep as many species as possible alive. Plants and animals (including humans) depend on each other for survival.

b Agree: Technology has already solved many environmental problems. It may provide the solutions to reversing global warming and it can help us to access renewable energy resources such as wind, sun and sea.
Disagree: Technology is not the answer to all our problems. We need to begin to think in a completely different way in order to stop exploiting the earth's resources and causing irreversible damage to the planet.

c Agree: Genetically modified crops can supply the world with a steady and sufficient quantity of food, because they can withstand disease and drought. There is no danger in growing genetically modified plants – people have been modifying crops for hundreds of years through breeding and grafting.
Disagree: Genetically modified crops are a dangerous experiment which could threaten the supply and diversity of current food crops. There is already enough food to go round if we waste less and change our eating habits and convert animal grazing land to food crop production.

d Agree: The generation of nuclear power involves little or no production of carbon dioxide gases (the main cause of global warming) and produces large quantities of electricity from a relatively small input of natural resources. Other fuels, such as coal and gas, cause high levels of air pollution and only exist in very limited quantities.
Disagree: Nuclear power has the potential to be the most polluting of all fuels, as nuclear radiation can cause widespread damage to a vast area and directly attacks the human body. It is extremely difficult to safely decommission (shut down) a nuclear reactor. The cleanest fuels are undoubtedly wind, sun and water; these renewable resources are becoming more efficient fuel sources as technology develops.

Taking a view

3 Key

It is the responsibility of individuals to change their lifestyle to prevent further damage.

5

Make sure students read the Note and explain that it is best to avoid making a statement in a composition that cannot be backed up by examples or reasons.

Possible answers

a Specific examples

a Restrictions and incentives are required for industry: Restrictions could be imposed on the level of greenhouse emissions from factories, the quantities of packaging materials used, and the use of non-renewable resources. Incentives such as grants and tax breaks could be introduced for the use of recycled materials and renewable energy resources.

b People could take fewer long-distance holidays: Non-essential air travel could be limited to a figure such as 2,000 km per person per year. A substantial energy tax on air fuel could be imposed to make long-distance air travel less attractive.

c Greener modes of transport should be promoted: Campaigns could be devised to encourage more cycling. Electric trams could be introduced to replace buses and trains. Massive grant and tax incentives could be introduced for the design and production of cars fueled by electric cells, hydrogen or bio-diesel.

d International agreements are required: Governments need to agree on things like the acceptable levels of emission of greenhouse gases, and the proportion of recycling of industrial and household waste.

e Individuals should ensure that their houses or flats are energy-efficient: Major savings in energy can be achieved through effective insulation, draught proofing, and the use of low-energy appliances.

f Businesses need to take a broader view rather than just working for profit: The hidden costs of waste, use of non-renewable resources, etc. need to be considered.

g We should buy fewer electrical labour-saving devices: Dishwashers, washing machines and vacuum cleaners all use a considerable amount of energy; we could do without some of them and complete these jobs by hand.

h People should get out of their cars: The alternatives such as walking, cycling and public transport are healthier and less polluting.

i The scientific evidence for climate change is unreliable and should not be believed: Any scientifically proven increase in global temperatures could be part of natural fluctuations. Such fluctuations have occurred throughout the history of the planet.

j There's no point in looking for a solution to this problem. It's already too late: Global warming is well underway, the planet is already unable to cope with the levels of greenhouse gases, which are continuing to rise, and the catastrophic results of this have already been shown by recent meteorological disasters around the globe.

b Consequences of taking action

a Restrictions and incentives for industry: The technology involved in production processes would change. There would be less waste and the demand for renewable resources would increase leading to investment in these areas.

b People could take fewer long-distance holidays: The tourist industry would decline possibly leading to some overseas tour operators going out of business. The domestic market would increase with short breaks. People may invest more time in other leisure activities at home.

c Greener modes of transport should be promoted: The demand for public transport would increase and vehicle manufacturers would have to produce greener vehicles. The demand for bikes would also increase. New manufacturers may emerge if the old ones don't adapt.

d International agreements are required: The rate of change would increase. Businesses would feel more secure in making decisions about investments.

e Individuals should ensure that their houses or flats are energy-efficient: There would be decrease in demand for gas and electricity as well as oil and solid fuel, but an increase in demand for insulating materials. People would have to make sure they didn't use appliances wastefully.

f Businesses need to take a broader view rather than just working for profit: Profits may fall, but the links between business and the community may become stronger.

g We should buy fewer electrical labour-saving devices: The demand for non-essential electrical goods would decline. People may spend a bit more time doing household tasks or find other ways of doing them.

h People should get out of their cars: Traffic congestion and pollution would decrease and people would be fitter.

i The scientific evidence for climate change is unreliable and should not be believed: Pollution and congestion would get worse. If it later proved that climate change is happening, it would be too late to make the necessary changes.

j There is no point looking for a solution to this problem: The problem would increase more and more rapidly.

c Consequences of not taking action

The case of not taking action is that pollution would increase. More and more people would die in extreme climatic conditions, such as droughts and hurricanes. There would come a point when it would be too late to reverse the processes.

6 Key

a Governments and individuals should take joint responsibility for the problem.

b, c Main argument 1: Industry produces most of the greenhouse gases, and this can only be controlled by government action.
Examples: Measures to discourage pollution, e.g. limiting or taxing the use of fossil fuels. Subsidies to encourage cleaner production processes.
Reason: businesses would see that pollution is a financial issue.

Main argument 2: Discussion between governments is necessary to ensure that solutions are successful.
Example: the Kyoto agreement.
Reason: efforts to reduce fuel consumption won't be successful without it.

Main argument 3: National and international policies will only succeed if individuals change their lifestyles.
Examples: people can reduce energy use in the home, e.g. by installing energy-efficient appliances or solar panels.
Reason: individuals can make a real difference.

Main argument 4: Individual attitudes to transport need to change.
Examples: individuals can walk, cycle or go by bus instead of using the car.
Reason: cars are a major source of the problem.

7 Key

Smoking should be banned in all public places.

8 Make sure students read the Note. Tell them to form a clear opinion in response to the topic: this could be agreement, disagreement or partial agreement.

Possible answers

Agree
Main arguments:
1 Health is the most important factor that affects our quality of life.
2 Smoking-related health problems cost the state, and therefore the tax payer, a huge amount of money.
3 It is an infringement of people's rights to put them in situations where their health is unnecessarily put at risk.
4 Public places will become much more pleasant environments to be in without cigarette smoke.
Supporting ideas:
1 Without good health we cannot enjoy our lives properly. Reducing both smokers and non-smokers exposure to smoking will improve everyone's health.
2 Banning smoking in public places would reduce the amount of money spent on doctor's fees,

hospital bills and insurance. It would also reduce the significant cost of lost working days.
3 Non-smokers have a right to breathe clean air.
4 In countries where smoking is banned on buses and trains, in cinemas and theatres, pubs and restaurants most people, including smokers, say they now prefer these environments.

Disagree
Main arguments:
1 It is an infringement of people's rights to prevent them from smoking.
2 The health risks to non-smokers caused by smoking in public places is unproven.
3 Smoking provides pleasure and relaxation to a large number of people. It is unfair to deprive them of this.
Supporting ideas:
1 We don't stop people from drinking alcohol, climbing dangerous mountains or driving fast cars, so we shouldn't try to stop them smoking. It is an example of government interfering in people's private lives, rather than allowing responsible adults to make their own decisions.
2 The effects of passive smoking would need to be investigated further to prove that there is a health risk to non-smokers.
3 If a smoking ban was introduced, many people would be unable to enjoy using public places. Businesses, such as pubs, restaurants and cinemas could lose money if smokers stopped using them.

Help yourself page 32

The final page in each unit is intended to raise a variety of extra areas that students can explore and to encourage responsibility for their own language learning.

Global issues

2 This exercise is intended to provide some thought-provoking ideas on the various topics. There are no right answers.

4 All of these sources can be useful for providing information on global issues.

IELTS to do list

Encourage the students to tick one of the boxes and plan to do this task outside class.

Where to look

Students can use these practical tips to find further information.

3 Fitness and health

Introduction page 33

Issues – This section introduces the overall theme of the unit, touching on both individual responsibility for health and the potential benefits and risks of scientific medicine.

Aims – Students are given opportunities to think and speak about broad health issues, learning relevant vocabulary along the way.

1 Ask students to work in pairs or groups to discuss photos 1–4.

Possible answers

a Photo 1 relates to oriental approaches to fitness that see being healthy as a combination of physical, mental, and spiritual well-being.
Photo 2 relates to the common use of gyms, both for overall physical fitness and also to look good.
Photo 3 relates to the treatment of illness through drugs and other medicines which people can easily buy over the counter in supermarkets or other shops.
Photo 4 relates to diet and its impact on health, including the consumption of health foods, organic foods, and vegetarianism.

b Tai Chi in Photo 1 might be beneficial in relieving tension and stress. A drawback might be that it requires time, practice, and dedication.
Gyms in Photo 2 might be beneficial because they are easy to access and provide a variety of exercise types. Drawbacks include possible overtraining and the enclosed environment. They can also be expensive.
Drugs and other medicines in Photo 3 might be beneficial in providing rapid relief from illness. Drawbacks might be side-effects and over use.
Health food in Photo 4 might be beneficial in preventing illness in later life. Drawbacks include the food's lack of appeal to some people. Health food products can also be expensive.

c Students may select from the photos or present their own ideas.

d It could be argued that any way of staying healthy might be dangerous if taken to extremes. For example, a determination to eat healthily might become obsessive, leading to dietary disorders. Also, participation in sport can lead to improved health but often runs risks, either due to lack of fitness or the possibility of injury.

e Dangers to health commonly reported in the media include those caused by lifestyle. Among these are the increased incidence of obesity amongst people of all ages, and the illnesses caused by the consumption of alcohol, cigarettes and illegal drugs. In addition, new diseases may emerge as viruses mutate, as happens with flu viruses.

f At this point students should be encouraged to come up with their own suggestions, although suggested answers are given in the headlines in 2.

2 Key

a cure	e transplant
b vaccination	f repair
c implants	g cloning
d explore	h regrows

3 Ask students to work in pairs or groups to discuss questions a–c.

Key

a–c All the breakthroughs are still potential. The wording of the headlines cover broad areas such as all cancers whereas the technology behind them at the moment is limited and specific. Some breakthroughs such as the use of face transplants for cosmetic reasons and human cloning are unlikely to ever be widespread for ethical reasons.

Reading page 34

Issues – This section introduces the placebo effect and makes a comparison between conventional and alternative medicine.

Aims – Students learn how read for gist and overall text structure in order to identify where answers are located. Students also learn how to find textual evidence in order to distinguish between *yes / no / not given* responses.

Orientation

1 Possible answers

a Conventional medicine offers physical explanations for illness and is based on scientific methods. Alternative medicine offers a broader range of explanations for illness, including mental and spiritual causes. However, the theories used to explain the effects of some alternative approaches are questioned by scientists.

b Conventional: anaesthetist, doctor, physician, rheumatologist, surgeon
Alternative: acupuncturist, aromatherapist, complementary practitioner, herbalist
An acupuncturist treats physical and emotional illnesses by applying needles to specific points in the body.
An anaesthetist gives anaesthetic (a drug which causes temporary unconsciousness) before an operation.
An aromatherapist uses essential oils to provide relaxation and treat minor physical illnesses.
A complementary practitioner is anyone who works in the field of alternative medicine.
A doctor is a trained practitioner of conventional medicine.
A herbalist uses plants and substances derived from plants to treat illnesses.
A physician is a doctor, especially one who is a specialist in general medicine.
A rheumatologist is a doctor who specializes in problems involving muscles and joints.
A surgeon is a doctor who specializes in medical operations which involve cutting open the body.

Text structure

2 Exercise 2 is intended to illustrate the importance of recognizing structure within IELTS passages. This can provide a useful map for finding the location of answers. Make sure students read the Note before they complete the exercise.

Key

A This section starts at the beginning of the text with the words *Want to devise a new form of alternative medicine?* …

B This section starts at the beginning of the third paragraph with the words *Placebos are treatments that* …

C This section starts at the beginning of the eighth paragraph with the words *The question is whether* …

Finding evidence

3 Exercise 3 is intended to illustrate the importance of finding evidence to distinguish between *false* and *not given* information. Make sure students read the Note before they complete the exercise.

Key

a, b In line 9, the writer advises new therapists to *make them pay you out of their own pockets*. This suggests the writer disagrees with the statement that *Alternative therapists should give free treatment*.

c, d There is no mention of *young people* in section A of the text. Consequently, there is no information given in the passage about the statement *Alternative therapy is particularly popular among young people*.

IELTS practice
Questions 1–5: Yes / No / Not given

Key

1 Yes. The writer suggests that it could *earn you a living. A good living* (line 17).

2 No. The writer, referring to illnesses that *get better on their own*, says *some of the improvement really would be down to you*, i.e. because of your treatment (line 22).

3 No. This cannot be true as *any mention of placebo is a touchy subject … tantamount to a charge of charlatanism* for many alternative practitioners (lines 33–38).

4 Not given. There is no mention by the writer of whether alternative practitioners are involved in surgical operations.

5 Yes. The examples of emotions given by the writer are *anger* (line 44) and *sadness* (line 45), which produce reddening of the face and crying, respectively.

Questions 6–10: True / False / Not given

Key

6 True. The text refers to *direct proof* that the pain-relief from placebos is brought about *at least in part* by natural endorphins (lines 63–65).

7 False. This is contradicted by *most people can't achieve placebo pain relief simply by willing it* (lines 66–67).

8 Not given. There are references to the greater effectiveness of red and blue medicines, but nothing about their sales.

9 False. The text first contradicts this by saying *Physicians who adopt a warm, friendly and reassuring bedside manner* are *more effective* (lines 78–83). Later, this is reinforced by saying that a professor of surgery who guarantees to solve your problems is *still unrivalled as a source of placebo power* (lines 115–119).

10 Not given. Cost is not mentioned in relation to integrating alternative and conventional medicine.

Exploration

4 Key

a *Do you* .... By omitting this the author creates a more informal / conversational tone.

b All these phrases are examples of forces which have not been identified by scientific study. Knowing their exact meaning is not necessary to understand the text. Rather, the author mentions them precisely because their meaning is vague and creates a mystical aura for these therapies.

c *But* could replace *yet*.

d *Charlatanism* is a synonym of *quackery*. Both words imply dishonesty.

e You would find *a trigger* on a gun. As a verb, it means *to cause or start*.

f The usual meaning of *recipe* is a list of instructions for cooking. *Ingredients* has the same association.

g *Face / faces* is a verb. The collocations are *face a problem* and *face a dilemma*.

5 Key

pain relief   blood vessels
touchy subject   bedside manner
healing power   strong hint

6 Key

a touchy subject   e strong hint
b blood vessels   f healing power
c pain relief   g placebo effect
d bedside manner

7 Possible answers

a States of mind may affect our physiology in many ways, e.g. stress may cause high blood pressure; excitement or concentration may allow distraction from pain.

Extra activity

Divide the class randomly into two. One half is to argue in favour of conventional medicine, the other half in favour of alternative medicine. Students work in pairs or groups. Give them five minutes to think up as many points as they can to support the view they have been given. At the end of five minutes each group pairs off with another group of the opposing view. Allow five minutes for them to debate their points.

Listening page 38

Aims – Students learn how to complete a matching lists activity and recognize the importance of identifying the number of options and listening for synonyms and similar phrases.

Orientation

1 Ask students to work in pairs or groups to discuss questions a–d.

Key

a Photo a: pitch
   Photo b: court
   Photo c: track
   Photo d: pool
   Photo e: rink

b pitch: football
   court: basketball
   track: running
   pool: swimming
   rink: ice hockey

c pitch: rugby, hockey
   court: tennis, badminton
   track: motor racing, cycling
   pool: water polo, diving
   rink: ice dance, speed skating

2 Ask students to work in pairs or groups to discuss questions a and b.

Synonyms

3 Exercise 3 is intended to emphasize that students should study the options and listen for associated clues, synonyms, and phrases in the recording. Make sure students read the Note, which underlines this learning point.

Possible answers

A injuries, hurt, cuts, bruises, sprains, medical, treat, treatment

B other people, meet, chat, socialize, eat, drink, café, bar

C lecture, rooms, halls, theatres, equipment, classes

D heat, steam, lose weight, sweat, kilos

E fit, test, check, prevent, heart, fat, lungs

F physiotherapist, treatment, prevention, muscles, tear, strain, massage

IELTS practice
Questions 1–6: Matching lists

Key

(1–3 in any order)	(4–6 in any order)
1 B	4 B
2 E	5 C
3 F	6 E

Recording script

Questions 1–6

Adam: Before we go on to look at specific sports, let's think for a moment about the non-sports facilities we really need here. Things like better changing rooms and showers.

Emma: Yes, if this really is going to be a state-of-the-art building it'll need to have hi-tech amenities but also **places for people to chill out after all the exercise they've been doing. Somewhere they can meet up for a drink or whatever afterwards** is essential in a place like this, but what else?

Adam: How about a sauna? Those who use them say it's the perfect way to relax after you've trained.

Emma: The trouble is, though, that there's a debate going on about how safe they are. Some say it's risky to be exposed to all that heat before or after strenuous exercise – which of course is exactly when people in sports centres want to use them. There have also been problems with people overusing them to sweat off weight. So to avoid any possible dangers, I don't think I'd include them on my list.

Adam: Talking of dangers, I wonder whether we ought to have some sort of facility where minor injuries like cuts and bruises and sprains can be treated?

Emma: Maybe. It would seem to make sense with all the mishaps that are bound to occur when you have so many people running and jumping about and so on. Ah. Hold on though: isn't the new medical centre going to be built right opposite?

Adam: Yes, it is. It should be finished by the end of next year.

Emma: Then there's no point, is there? Anyone who gets hurt can go over there, where there'll be much better treatment than anything we could offer on-site.

Adam: Yes, I can see that.

Emma: What we should provide, though, is **a facility with full-time physiotherapists**, for everybody on the campus that is. As well as treating people, they could work on prevention of things like muscle tears and strains.

Adam: Right.

Emma: And something else the new place ought to have, also as a way of preventing injuries, is **somewhere to test just how fit people** are before they start lifting weights or running long distances and so on.

Adam: Yes, I was going to suggest that. **When I was at the Newport centre they put me on a static bike to check out my cardiovascular system**, then they worked out how much body fat I had ... all of it valuable information, telling you exactly what shape you're in.

Emma: Another thing I've heard some universities do, especially some of the newer ones, is provide rooms and equipment for lectures to take place actually inside their sports centres. How do you feel about that?

Adam: Well as it happens I've got first-hand experience of that too. We **used to have some of our Sports Science lectures right next to the main sports hall**, and I think it made what we were hearing about seem much more relevant to the real world. So in that respect I definitely think it's a good idea, yes.

Emma: Hmm. I can see that, though my own feeling is that we need to have more concrete reasons. The problem is that we won't have unlimited space, and somehow I don't think providing more lecture halls is going to be one of our priorities. So I'd be against that one, I'm afraid. Anything else?

Adam: Well just that I agree about the need to have a **place where people can go for a chat** and maybe have a coffee or a bite to eat together. That was something I always thought was **one of the strong points of the centre in London**. It was a great place to find out about new activities from the people who actually did them.

4 Possible answers

A the centre, the gym, sports hall / complex, here, this place (we already know they are in the centre)

B on (the) campus, near the Students Union, halls of residence, science faculty

C in town, downtown, in the centre, off campus

7 tables

8 pool, swim

9 court

10 court

Questions 7–10: Classification

Key

7 B
8 C
9 A
10 B

Recording script

Questions 7–10

Adam: So what about the main sports facilities themselves? What do we need?

Emma: Well we don't need a rugby pitch because there's already one on the campus. The same's true of **table tennis**, really – **most of the halls of residence for students have their own tables**, so there's no point in using precious space here for any more.

Adam: Agreed. Something none of them have, though, is any sort of pool. A lot of students have complained about this, saying **they have to take a bus downtown if they want to go for a swim**.

Emma: Yes, that's definitely one for this place. Perhaps a Jacuzzi, too. That would be nice, wouldn't it?

Adam: It would. Perhaps **next to the squash courts, just down there to the right**. They're very popular, by the way. I think we should have a couple more here, don't you?

Emma: Absolutely. And another sport that's been growing in popularity is volleyball, especially since we did so well at the last Olympics.

Adam: Don't you mean **basketball**?

Emma: Yes, I do, sorry. Anyway, the point is that **there is a court in the old gym next to the Students Union building**, but it always seems to be fully booked up, even though it's not very good. And there's nowhere else on campus to play.

Adam: OK, let's have one of those, too. How much space have we got left, by the way?

Speaking page 40

Issues – This section introduces the theme of healthy eating.

Aims – Students learn the importance of extended answers for discussion questions in Speaking Part 3 and practise language for giving reasons.

Giving reasons

2 Exercise 2 is intended to introduce and practise the language for giving extended replies.

3 Key

1 False. Frozen fruit and vegetables can be just as nutritious as fresh and can contain more vitamin C if frozen immediately after picking.

2 b. Potatoes are a vegetable, but nutritionally they are more like starchy foods, such as rice and bread, so they do not count towards the recommended five fruits and vegetables a day.

3 b, d, e. Some biscuits are high in fat and sugar, and pastry and chips are also high in fat. Too much sugar and fat can contribute to weight gain, and may need to be reduced when trying to lose weight.

4 False. The calcium in milk is contained in the non-fat part of the milk, so removing fat from milk does not reduce the calcium content.

5 a, d, f

6 False. The starchy foods that we eat such as bread, rice, pasta, and potatoes provide us with an excellent source of energy, as well as many nutrients, so there is no need for us to take extra sugar in our diet.

4 Make sure students read the Note before they complete the exercise.

Language for writing page 41

Aims – Students revise features of relative clauses, and learn important structures for use in academic writing, such as combining relative pronouns with prepositions (*of which*) and with quantifiers (*several of which*).

1 Key

a A defining relative clause gives essential information, without it the main clause would have a different sense. (A non-defining relative clause adds extra information, but the main clause would have the same sense without it.)

b A non-defining relative clause is separated by commas.

c *That* can be used in defining relative clauses in place of *which* or *who*.

d The relative pronoun can sometimes be left out in defining relative clauses, but only when it is the object of the main verb. Compare the two example sentences: *chocolate is something (that) nearly everyone likes* (*that* can be omitted since it is the object (nearly everyone likes *that* [= *chocolate*]); *people that smoke normally damage their health* (*that* cannot be omitted since it is the subject of *smoke*).

2 Key

a Incorrect, add commas: My mother**,** who's a doctor**,** works in the maternity hospital.
b Incorrect, add *which*: Ligaments, **which** join bones in the human body, are made of strong tissue.
c Correct, although *that* or *who* can be added optionally: Do you know anyone **that** I can ask about this?
d Incorrect, add *who* / *that*: The pharmacist **who** gave me this medicine said it would help.
e Correct
f Incorrect, *that* cannot be used in a non-defining clause: Dr James, **who** has written several books on the subject, is a dietician.

3 Key

a The study, in which the Government had invested so much money, proved nothing.
b Darwin, on whose findings the theory was based, was the first to observe this.
c The people to whom the researchers spoke at length confirmed this.
d Crick's work on DNA, for which he received a Nobel Prize, transformed biology.
e Dr Fell is someone with whose ideas few scientists would disagree.
f Orion is the star from which light left hundreds of years ago.

4 Key

a The team found two fossils, neither of which was Triassic.
b The disease was caught by sixty-four people, most of whom recovered quickly.
c The examination was taken by 532 candidates, 43.4% of whom passed.
d We looked at many studies, several of which indicated the same pattern.
e The firm has appointed five new managers, all of whom are men.

Writing page 42

Orientation

1 Possible anwers

a Photo 1: children might have been eating healthier meals including more fruit and vegetables.
Photo 2: children might have been playing outdoors or reading books.
Photo 3: children might have been playing outdoors or reading books.
Photo 4: children might have been travelling to school on foot, or by bus or bicycle.
b Children have become less healthy in western countries, as shown by the prevalence of childhood obesity.

Organizing ideas

2 Key

a You have to write about the impact of eating and lifestyle on children's health.
b *Some people say this has had a negative effect on their* [children's] *health*.
c Students decide their own opinion.
d The answer depends on students' views in c. For example, a student that has no strong opinion may take a balanced approach, including arguments both for and against. However, this is not necessary.

3 Exercise 3 is intended to show that the choice of paragraph structure is related to the writer's opinion. Make sure students read the Note before they complete the exercise.

Key

a The writer has followed the first approach: arguments in favour of the opinion.
b The writer's opinion is stated in the first paragraph, second sentence.
c The first main paragraph (paragraph 2) deals with diet. The second main paragraph (paragraph 3) deals with exercise.

Using organizing expressions

4 Exercises 4 and 5 are intended to show the importance of the organizing expressions in the main paragraphs (2 and 3). Make sure students read the Note before they complete the exercise.

Key

Children increasingly eating in fast-food restaurants – *Secondly*

Children doing less exercise, at school – *(There is) also*

Children no longer walking or cycling to school – *To make matters worse*

Children staying at home, doing things which don't involve exercise – *Finally*

Individual changes not dangerous, but taken together they are – *To sum up*

5 Key

To begin with – First of all, In the first place

Secondly, Also, To make matters worse – Furthermore, Moreover, As well as that, For another thing

Finally – Lastly

To sum up – In conclusion

Think, plan, write

6 Encourage students to work through the stages in the Organizing ideas section and use their own opinions to decide what to include, then organize supporting arguments into groups for paragraphs.

7 Remind students to use the phrases in exercises 4 and 5.

Help yourself page 44

The final page in each unit is intended to raise a variety of extra areas that students can explore and to encourage responsibility for their own language learning.

Vocabulary

1 Key

a noun

b vocabularies

c on the 2nd syllable

d /vəˈkæbjələri/ and /vəˈkæbjələri/. In American English there is an extra syllable: the last but one syllable is pronounced as a full /e/ sound rather than /ə/.

e whether the word is countable [C] or uncountable [U]

f *Reading will increase your vocabulary; The word 'failure' was not in his vocabulary; When did the word 'bungalow' first enter the vocabulary?; The word has become part of advertising vocabulary.*

2 Possible answers

Trendy, cool, Cheers! and *clockwise* could all be active vocabulary. The first three are useful in everyday speech, while *clockwise* is precise and of practical use.

Voluminous and *anticyclonic* could be considered as passive vocabulary. It is easier to say *big* or *huge* than *voluminous*; *anticyclonic* is technical vocabulary.

3 Possible answers

1 Advantages: it's easy to look up the information. Disadvantages: there is no extra information about part of speech, how to use the words in context, etc.

2 Advantages: grouping words by part of speech may help students to use them appropriately. Disadvantages: it may be difficult to look up the information. There is no information on how to use the words in context.

3 Advantages: it may be easier to memorize words when they are recorded in the same context in which they were first learned. Disadvantages: words may be rather randomly grouped together, and there is no extra information about part of speech or how to use the words in context.

4 Advantages: words are contextualized in useful groups which may make them more memorable. Disadvantages: there is no information about part of speech or usage.

5 Advantages: detailed information is given, including fully contextualized examples. Disadvantages: it may be too time-consuming to record vocabulary in this way.

IELTS to do list

Encourage the students to tick one of the boxes and plan to do this task outside class.

Where to look

Students can use these practical tips to find further information.

4 The arts

Introduction page 45

Issues – This section introduces the theme of visual art with visual and textual material providing references to a wide range of styles from the history of art.

Aims – Students are given opportunities to respond to and discuss a range of visual art images and a description of the main historical artistic movements. They also discuss their own personal attitudes to and involvement in art.

1 Key

a Photo 1 shows handprints on a wall. (Cueva de los Manos, Patagonia, Argentina, circa 8000 BC.)
Photo 2 shows the goddess, Minerva pacifying a mythical beast, the centaur. (*Minerva Tames the Centaur*, Sandro Boticelli, 1482.)
Photo 3 shows kelp seaweed. (*Kelp Secrets*, Gerrit Greve, 1993–1996.)
Photo 4 shows a car breaking through a wall. (Graffiti art on the Berlin Wall, anonymous artist, 1988.)

b Oldest: Photo 1 (Circa 8000 BC)
Most modern: Photo 3 (1993–1996)

c Photo 1: South American cave dwellers, 10,000 years ago.
Photo 2: An Italian Renaissance painter (Boticelli).
Photo 3: A modern artist (Greve).
Photo 4: An anonymous graffiti artist.

d Photo 1: in a cave.
Photo 2: in an art gallery or museum.
Photo 3: in an art gallery, a private house, or a large business premises.
Photo 4: on an outside wall of a public building.

e Photo 1: This may possibly have been made as a message to other cave dwellers, or as a record of the people who lived there.
Photo 2: Renaissance painters usually produced their paintings for rich patrons.
Photo 3: The painter may have wanted to make money from the painting or simply used it as a form of artistic expression.
Photo 4: The artist wanted to make a political point, about the desire of East Germans to escape to the West.

2 Students read the text and answer the questions alone, before comparing answers with the whole class.

Key

a humorous, cynical

b He compares it to the effects of drinking alcohol, so he appears not to take it very seriously.

c Cave paintings: primitive art drawn on the walls of caves.
Church paintings: religious art, particularly popular in the Middle Ages.
Renaissance: fourteenth- to sixteenth-century art inspired by an interest in classical Greek and Roman civilizations.
Enlightenment: an eighteenth-century movement based on science and reason.
Romantic: a nineteenth-century movement based on strong feelings, imagination and nature.
Impressionism: a late nineteenth-century style which used dabs of colour to show the effects of light.
Expressionism: an early twentieth-century style that concentrated on showing people's feelings and emotions rather than showing objects in a realistic way.
Vorticism: a short-lived British movement of the early twentieth century, using bold lines and harsh colours.
Modern conceptual art: a movement starting in the 1960s and 1970s, where the ideas behind a work of art are given greater significance than the work itself.

Reading page 46

Issues – This section introduces the topic of installation art and public reaction to it.

Aims – Students learn the importance of text structure and how to work with question stems in answering multiple-choice questions.

Orientation

1 Ask students to work in pairs to discuss the photo.

Key

a The picture shows a work of art, displayed in a gallery. (*Installation S.R.* by Matti Brauns.) The ceiling of the exhibition room is mirrored in the water.

Style

2 Possible answers

a Installation art = a temporary work of art, using a variety of materials, such as sculpture, video, sound and performance.
Performance art = a type of art which is made up of the actions of an individual or group at a particular place and time.

b To make fun of the title of the work and perhaps the work itself, by suggesting that it is rather predictable.

c Perhaps not. It may just be a story made up by the writer to help make a point.

d humorous, mocking

Text structure

3 Key

What is installation art? Paragraphs 3–4
Why has it become so ubiquitous? Paragraphs 5–6
And why is it so irritating? Paragraph 7

Using question stems

4 Possible answers

a ... the public are unsure what modern art forms consist of.

b Because they are not officially recognized as art.

c None

d It marked the beginning of installation art. It also removed the idea that art involved taste, skill and craftmanship.

e ... want to find their own new ways of engaging audiences and installation art is the easiest way of doing this.

f ... are often too concerned with the intellectual history of art.

IELTS practice

Questions 1–6: Multiple-choice questions

Make sure students read the Note and remind them of the text structure that they identified in exercise 3.

Key

1 D. The men were both unsure whether the falling and collecting of the beads was itself art, and if so what branch of modern art it was. A is false because the text does not state or indicate that installations are unsophisticated. B is false because there is no suggestion that the woman's running was linked to the nature of the works. C may well be true, but the people picking up beads were helping the woman, not participating in art.

2 C. The text says *anything can be an installation so long as it has art status conferred on it*, which *the flashing fluorescent tube in your kitchen* doesn't have because it is not recognized by the art establishment (lines 34–36). A is false because the text talks about an installation in which *lights went on and off in a gallery* (line 5), and the dictionary definition says *either outdoors or indoors* (line 28). B is false because, although the dictionary definition *rules out paintings, sculptures*, this by itself is not sufficient to say that domestic lights are not installation art. D is not necessarily true, and is not relevant to the definition of installation art.

3 D. The text says *They* (i.e. installations) *do not all share a set of essential characteristics* (lines 46–47). A is false, because the text says *some* – not all – *will be site-specific* (line 48). B is false because it says *some*, but not all, *will demand audience participation* (lines 47–48). C is false because *some*, not all, *will be conceptual jokes* (line 49).

4 A. The text says *There have been installations since Marcel Duchamp put a urinal in a New York gallery in 1917* (lines 53–55) and that *This was the most resonant gesture in twentieth-century art* (line 55–56). B is false because there is no indication that other artists at the time were angry. C is false because the text talks of the item *discrediting notions of taste, skill and craftsmanship* (lines 56–57), which suggests it was not a particularly well-made object. D is false because the text suggests it brought about a change in attitudes to what constituted art, rather than showing what it was not.

5 B. Foster speaks of artists *using their work as a terrain on which to evoke feelings or provoke reactions* (lines 70–71) and says they *can more easily explore what concerns them* (line 76–77). A is false because Foster states that *with installations there is less pressure to conform to the demands of a formal tradition* (lines 74–76). C is false because he describes a different approach used by modern artists, but does not suggest that they find these any easier.

D is false because he says ... *photography, painting or sculpture can do the same* (evoke feelings or provoke reactions: lines 72–73).

6 C. The text describes *installation artists* as being *frequently so bound up with the intellectual history of art and its various 'isms' that they forget that those who are not educated in this neither care nor understand* (lines 81–85). A is not suggested. B is false because, as above, the text describes *installation artists* as being *bound up with the intellectual history of art and its various 'isms'*. D is not stated in the text, and the statement *in the many cases when craftsmanship is removed* (lines 79–80) in fact suggests the opposite.

Questions 7–11: Short-answer questions

Key

7 Thanks for that (line 24)
8 (about) 50% / fifty percent (line 90)
9 downstairs (line 101)
10 moved (line 105)
11 (you) the spectator (lines 106–107)

Question 12: Global multiple-choice

Key

12 B. The writer struggles to find a suitable definition, and eventually gives up, but concludes in the final paragraph by describing a work that is challenging and worthwhile. A is false because the writer refers several times to the growing public interest in installations. C is false because the writer says that installation artists are often concerned with the intellectual history of art, but doesn't state that it is necessary to understand art history in order to appreciate installation art. D is false because the writer does not indicate this, nor suggest any criteria for comparing the quality of differing art forms.

Exploration

5 Key

a	to	f	in
b	to	g	to
c	on	h	of
d	in	i	up
e	of	j	of

6 Key

a 4   b 3   c 1   d 2

7 These questions are intended to encourage students to respond personally to issues raised by and related to the text.

Listening   page 50

Aims – Students learn how to use expressions of sequence, direction, naming and number as clues when answering questions involving labelling a diagram.

Orientation

1 Key

a Photo 1: a woodwind instrument, something like a clarinet.
Photo 2: a large percussion instrument, a type of drum.

b Photo 1: they are being used in some type of ceremony, possibly a religious one.
Photo 2: they are being used as part of a street parade.

f The instrument is the bagpipes. It is often associated with Scotland, although similar instruments are used worldwide.

Diagrams and descriptions

2 Key

4, 1, 3, 2

3 Make sure students read the Note before they complete the exercise.

Key

sequence: *in addition, then, this causes*
direction: *along, downwards, outwards*
naming: *or..., called the, known as*
number: *there are three of these, usually has nine*

4 Key

1 blowpipe
2 chanter
3 drones

IELTS practice
Questions 1–5: Labelling a diagram

Key

1	mouthpiece	4 bell
2	valves	5 water key
3	finger buttons	

IELTS practice
Questions 6–10: Note completion

Key

6	3,500 years	9 small
7	eighteenth	10 French horn
8	loud and clear	

Recording script

The trumpet is quite a remarkable instrument. Take the B-flat type for instance, the kind of trumpet most people use today. If we stretched one out in a straight line, it would measure nearly 140 centimetres in length. What we see in the diagram, then, is a very long brass tube wrapped around itself in order to save space. To produce its characteristic sound, the musician blows continuously into **the small metal cup on the left called the mouthpiece**, which is shaped to fit the lips. The air travels along the lead pipe and round the tuning slide, which can be moved in or out to change the instrument's pitch. The air then reaches the feature that distinguishes the trumpet from, for instance, a bugle: **the three valves that extend from above the top to below the bottom of the instrument**. Each valve can send the air flow one of two ways: either along the main pipe, the shortest route, or else into an extra length of tube, thus lowering the pitch of the sound being played. The musician does this by pressing one of **the finger buttons** at the top, diverting the air into the first tube if the first is pressed, into the second – and shortest – by using the second, or into the longest one – the third – by pressing number three. The air then continues its way round the bend in the lead pipe and along to the end at **the widest part of the body, known as the bell**, which projects the powerful sound forwards. Incidentally, all this breath forced through the metal of the instrument does of course contain water vapour, and this will start to condense and form droplets after a certain amount of playing. The result is a 'gurgling' sound from the trumpet, so to avoid this there is **a device on the tuning slide called the water key**, which, when pressed, lets the water drip out.

The trumpet, in one form or another, has been around for a long time. The earliest type we have actual proof of was a short, straight instrument used with marching soldiers by the ancient Egyptians' eighteenth Dynasty, which makes it **three thousand five hundred years old**, although other cultures in China and Peru certainly had something similar very early on. This use of the trumpet in military contexts, as well as at ceremonial occasions, was to continue through the times of the ancient Greeks and Romans, but it wasn't until the seventeenth century that it became a genuinely popular instrument, at least in the West. **At the beginning of the eighteenth century it was finally accepted as part of the typical orchestra**, and the addition of valves in the nineteenth century, making it much more versatile, consolidated its position as a major orchestral instrument. Nowadays **the sound of the trumpet, which is of course both loud and clear**, means that for many pieces it is used to lead the brass section of the orchestra. This sound, and its versatility, have helped extend its use to other forms of music such as jazz and pop, but there is another, very practical, reason for its widespread popularity. In comparison with many others such as the tuba, the cello, or even the trombone, **it is a fairly small instrument** that can easily be transported and played just about anywhere. The downside of all this popularity, though, is that as everyone wants to be a trumpeter it can be difficult for the young musician looking for work to find a vacancy. As a result, it's often the case that **quite a few of the French horn players in a modern orchestra actually began their musical careers as trumpet players**.

Speaking page 52

Aim – Students learn to use a variety of phrases to introduce a Part 2 Speaking topic.

Orientation

1 Key

Speaker 1: Photo 4   Speaker 3: Photo 2
Speaker 2: Photo 1   Speaker 4: Photo 3

Recording script

Speaker 1: **I've decided to talk about** *Billy Elliot*, which I saw at the Victoria Palace Theatre a while ago. The musical, that is, not the film, which I still haven't seen. Anyway, it's about a boy who wants to be a ballet dancer, but everything and everyone – except his teacher – seems to be against him. It's a good story, and the dancing and singing are brilliant.

Speaker 2: **There are a lot that I've enjoyed, but the best one was** last year's Cambridge Folk Festival. There were musicians from all over the world and all sorts of music, like gospel and salsa. The atmosphere was great too, and there was a real mix of people. My own particular favourite was a Celtic band, who did some traditional stuff but with a modern beat.

Speaker 3: **My favourite was** an outdoor performance of Shakespeare's *Macbeth*, which I saw at Wenlock Priory in July. It's such a dark play, with witches and ghosts and murder. It was the perfect setting. The best thing of all was the way the evening gradually got darker as the end of the play approached, with the ruins of the church towering over the stage. Perfect for an ending like that.

Speaker 4: **I remember one** film which was

perhaps the best I've seen: the *Lord of the Rings*. I'd read the book and I thought nobody could ever make a movie of it, but Peter Jackson, the director, did a fantastic job. OK, some parts of the book, and a few characters, have been left out, but there's so much attention to detail that you hardly notice, even in a film that lasts three hours.

Getting started

2 Make sure that students read the Note.

Key

Speaker 1: b   Speaker 3: a
Speaker 2: d   Speaker 4: c

3 Tell students to think about what they are going to say for a minute or two and then take turns to talk about the events they have attended.

IELTS practice
Part 2: Extended speaking

4 Remind students to write down only brief notes (not full sentences) and not to miss out any of the items on the card.

Extra activity

Tell students to time their partner's talk and give brief feedback. Write the following headings on the board and tell them to comment on these areas: *Good timing? Clear and easy to follow? Any grammatical errors?*

5 Students work in pairs. Ask them to time each other if possible and make a note of how long their partner spoke for.

Language for Writing page 53

Aim – Students practise the correct use of tenses to describe trends. This will be particularly useful for Writing Task 1.

Choosing tenses

1 Key

go up: rise (rose, risen)
grow (grew, grown)
increase (increased, increased)

go down: fall (fell, fallen)
decrease (decreased, decreased)
decline (declined, declined)
drop (dropped, dropped)

2 Key

a past simple   d future simple
b present continuous   e future perfect
c present perfect

3 Key

a trend happening now: present continuous
a predicted trend: future simple
a trend happening before a future date: future perfect
a trend up to now: present perfect
a trend in the past: past simple

4 Key

past simple: last October, before 2000, over the previous decade, during the summer of 2003
present perfect: since 1998, up to now, so far this century, for the last six months
present continuous: at present, currently, nowadays, at the moment
future simple: in the year after next, between 2015 and 2020
future perfect: in five years' time, by 2025

Extra activity

Write the following expressions on the board: *Since 2001 ... , At the moment ... , During the winter of 2004 ... , In ten years' time ... , Next year ... .* Ask students to write five complete sentences about themselves starting with these expressions. Students swap answers with a partner to check accurate use of tenses.

5 Possible answers

a fell / declined / decreased / dropped
b will have risen / will have increased / will have grown
c is not rising / is not falling
d have fallen / have declined / have decreased / have dropped
e rose / increased / grew
f increased ... decreased / grew ... dropped
g will have risen / will have increased / will have grown
h will have declined

6 Possible answers

Adult fiction is forecast to drop another three per cent by 2010.
Audio-visual is expected to increase three per cent from 2010 to 2015.
Adult non-fiction is predicted neither to rise nor fall between 2005 and 2010.

Writing page 54

Aims – Students learn to use a range of vocabulary for describing trends and learn to use approximate phrases when describing figures.

Orientation

1 Possible answers

b More popular: recorded music, live music, cinema, musicals
Less popular: theatre, opera, reading, ballet
(Note: these answers will vary in different cultures.)

Describing trends

2 Key

a The vertical axis relates to the average household expenditure on books, music, cinema and theatre in Australia, in dollars per week.
The horizontal axis gives to the time period, 1984 to 1999.
b The lines represent the amount of expenditure for each category (books, recorded music, cinema and live music and theatre) over the given time period.
c *The graph shows* the average household expenditure, in dollars per week, on selected cultural items in Australia during the period 1984 to 1999.
d Books: fall, decline, drop, go down, decrease
Recorded music: rise, increase, go up, grow
Cinema: fall, increase, recover, fluctuate

3 Make sure students read the Note before they complete the exercise.

Key

a declined slightly
b fell steadily
c dropped sharply
d fluctuated
e increase
f rose rapidly
g went up
h recovered steadily

4 Possible answer

There was a slight decline in the expenditure on books at first, a steady fall over the next five years and then a sharp drop in the final period.

5 Possible answer

Overall statistics show that Australians spent rather more on films and recorded music, about the same on the performing arts, but a lot less on books in 1999 than in 1984.

Describing figures

6 Make sure students read the Note before they complete the exercise.

Key

a Art values fell by just under ten per cent. / There was a fall of nearly ten per cent in art values.
b Since January, cinema audiences have gone up by just over 20,000. / There has been a rise in cinema audiences of approximately 20,000.
c Currently, the market for prints is growing by nearly a third each year. / Currently, there is growth of roughly 33% in the market for prints.

Think, plan, write

7 Key

a The vertical axis relates to the percentage of the total population who go to the cinema in Britain once or more a month.
The horizontal axis relates to the time period, 1984 to 2002.
b The lines represent different age groups: under 14, 15–24, 25–34, 35 and over.
c There was a rise in all age groups over the period 1984 to 2002.
The growth rate was steadiest for the over 35s, while there were more peaks and troughs for the other age groups.
The most frequent cinema goers were those in the 15–24 age group throughout the period.
With the exception of the under 14s and the 25–34 age groups in 1991 and 1997 the age groups maintained their position relative to other groups.

8 Remind students to use a good range of vocabulary to describe trends and to give approximate figures where appropriate. Remind them also of the points they learnt in Unit 1: use a simple, accurate description to introduce their writing, and select the main features.

Help yourself page 56

The final page in each unit is intended to raise a variety of extra areas that students can explore and to encourage responsibility for their own language learning.

Reading more widely

1 This exercise is intended to raise students' awareness of different possible approaches to improving their reading skills. There are no right answers.

2 Key

closest to IELTS: a, b, d, e
would probably never appear: c, f

3 All of these suggestions may prove useful to students.

IELTS to do list

Encourage the students to tick one of the boxes and plan to do this task outside class.

Where to look

Students can use these practical tips to find further information.

5 Work and business

Introduction page 57

Issues – This section introduces the theme of work, focusing on types of job and the qualities needed to run your own business.

Aims – Students learn some of the vocabulary of job sectors, and discuss personal qualities in relation to running a business.

1 Check that students know the meaning of *retail* (selling direct to the public) and *service* (a business whose work involves doing something for customers but not producing goods, e.g. banking, advertising, tourism).

Key

a Photo 1: manufacturing   Photo 4: service
   Photo 2: retail   Photo 5: creative
   Photo 3: business   Photo 6: technical

b Photos 1 (welding), 5 (tailoring / dress design) and 6 (scientist) are all skilled jobs.
   Photos 2 (shop assistant) and 4 (call centre staff) are unskilled.
   Photo 1 (welding) is a manual job.
   Photo 4 (call centre staff) is the closest to a clerical job. These are office based.

2 Make sure students write down their own answers before comparing with a partner.

Reading page 58

Issues – This section introduces the the topic of the role of work in our lives.

Aims – Students learn to identify key words in sentence completion tasks, and practise locating the source of a summary.

Orientation

1 Ask students to work alone, before comparing answers with a partner. Check that students know the meaning of *maternity leave* (a break from work taken when a woman has a baby) and *sabbatical* (an extended break from work, often to study or travel).

Extra activity

Students work in groups. Ask them to come up with as many more ideas as they can to add to the list in Exercise 1. Make a list on the board of the suggestions and ask students to vote on the most important. Ask each student in turn to give a reason for their choice and then take a second vote to see if students have changed their views.

Possible suggestions: a good boss, promotion opportunities, opportunities to travel, perks, e.g. company car, shares, etc., flexible hours, variety of tasks, plenty of responsibility, ongoing training and development, convenient location, pleasant working environment.

Reading for gist

2 Check that students know the meaning of *myth* (something that many people believe, but which is not true).

Key

The writer thinks that work is good for you.
(... 'Work' as Albert Einstein said, 'is the only thing that gives substance to life.*)

Key words

3 Key

Topic words:
   a problem (noun)
   b time off (noun)
Content words:
   a blamed (verb), work (noun)
   b companies (noun), childbirth (noun)

4 Key

a *Work has become the scapegoat for all our woes* (line 5) (problem = woes, blamed = scapegoat)
b *a lot of firms offer longer maternity leave* (line 13) (companies = firms, time off = leave, childbirth = maternity)

5 Make sure students read the Note before they complete the exercise.

Key

1 press, work
2 study, job satisfaction
3 workforce, British
4 length, working day
5 Marx, work
6 present-day, cause, alienation, work
7 romantic involvement, colleague

IELTS practice

Questions 1–7: Sentence completion

Key

1 L. The text says *Pick up any newspaper ... and you'll read about how work is killing our marriages ...* (lines 1–3)
2 J. The second paragraph says *more than in France, Germany, Italy or Spain* (lines 11–12).
3 D. The text refers to *two-thirds [of] staff* being allowed to *work from home some of the time* (lines 14–16).
4 I. The second paragraph says *the working day has increased in length over the last two decades* but by *just one minute and forty-two seconds* (lines 17–19).
5 G. In the third paragraph, Marx is quoted as saying that work *mortifies* [the worker's] *body* (line 32).
6 C. The writer talks of *relentless negativity about work* (line 33), before concluding paragraph 3 by saying *If we accept that work is dull and demeaning ... we are allowing alienation to remain* (line 38).
7 F. The fourth paragraph states that *two-thirds of us have dated someone at work* (line 44).

Finding text

6 Key

Paragraphs 4–6

IELTS practice

Questions 8–12: Summary completion

Key

8 B relationships (line 41)
9 F identity (line 48)
10 E choice (line 58)
11 H children (line 71)
12 A leisure (line 83)

Exploration

7 Key

a workers are satisfied
b of firms
c the average working day has increased
d work is
e put in
f the question
g invest
h seeing work as

8 Key

a the people
b like something / it
c get
d the distinction between work and leisure
e abandon the notion of work as a down payment on life
f modern myths

Listening page 62

Aims – Students learn to predict answers and compare them with what they actually hear in a listening. They also practise listening out for prepositions of place to help follow directions.

Orientation

1 Ask students to work in pairs or groups to discuss photos 1–3.

Possible answers

a Photo 1: waitress; serve customers in a restaurant / café
   Photo 2: research assistant; collect, analyse and present information
   Photo 3: office worker; use a computer, prepare documents
b Photo 1: communication skills
   Photo 2: organizational skills, communication skills
   Photo 3: organizational skills, communication skills
c Photo 1: patience, energy, punctuality, honesty
   Photo 2: intelligence, energy, creativity
   Photo 3: organizational skills, communication skills
   adjectives: intelligent, creative, patient, punctual, experienced, honest, energetic

IELTS practice

Questions 1–5: Multiple-choice questions

1 Make sure students read the Note before they complete the exercise. Remind them to choose the answers only on the basis of what they actually hear.

Key

1. B. Steve asks *what the work actually consists of*. It cannot be A as he says he's *looking for a summer job, not long-term employment*. He says the wages are in the advertisement, so it is not C.

2. C. Ellen says *there've been a few who didn't find it easy to get there on time in the morning*, and also refers to *punctuality*. She says that they've *always found students to be honest*, so A is false, and that they have *the basic IT skills needed*, making B also false.

3. A. Ellen says *most callers would be people wanting to check the balance on their cards*. She also says that people ring another number for lost or stolen cards, so B and C are false.

4. A. Ellen mentions the *change in the number of women*, adding that *nowadays they make up around 55% of the total*. The figure for men of *three-quarters*, or 75%, relates to the past, and to card holders, not callers.

5. B. Ellen says Steve's intelligent, adding *which of course you need to be*. A is false because Steve asks what kind of experience is needed, but Ellen replies *none really*. The supervisors are described as helpful, not the operatives, so C is also false.

Recording script

Questions 1–5

Ellen:	Hello, Top Job Employment Agency. Ellen Sykes speaking. How can I help you?
Steve:	Good morning, my name's Steve Collins and I'm calling about the call centre job advertised in today's paper.
Ellen:	For an operative handling credit card enquiries?
Steve:	Yes, that's right. The wages and working conditions are all in the ad, so **what I'd like to know now is what the work actually consists of**. I should explain that I'm a student looking for a summer job, not long-term employment.
Ellen:	That's OK. The people at InterCard say they've always found students to be honest, which of course is essential in this line of work, and they have the basic IT skills needed there. Apparently **there have been a few who didn't find it easy to get there on time in the morning**, but in most cases their punctuality is as good as anybody else's! Anyway, about the work, and I know a bit about this because as it happens I've worked there myself.
Steve:	Really?
Ellen:	Yes, for about a year. You'd find that **most callers would be people wanting to check the balance on their cards, query payments made and so on**.

Steve:	And from those who've had their cards stolen?
Ellen:	No, they ring another number for that: an emergency line. People also call that number if they lose their cards.
Steve:	And what are most callers like? I mean, what kind of people are they?
Ellen:	All sorts, really. All ages, every kind of background. Though one definite trend is the change in the number of **women**. Nowadays **they make up around 55% of the total**, whereas years ago there used to be a majority of men calling. At one time, I heard, as many as three-quarters of all credit cards were actually held by men, but that must have been long before I was there.
Steve:	It's certainly different now. So to do this job, what sort of experience do I need?
Ellen:	None really. Have you got a credit card yourself?
Steve:	Yes, I have.
Ellen:	Then you probably know quite a bit about them already, and as a student **you're obviously intelligent, which of course you need to be for the job**. So after a day or so working with an experienced operative I'm sure you'll have picked up enough to deal with routine enquiries, which of course most of them are.
Steve:	But there are bound to be questions I can't deal with, at least at first. What happens then?
Ellen:	In that case you can ask a supervisor. They're very helpful to new staff.
Steve:	I think I like the sound of this. What do I do next?

Predicting

3 Key

a The names of buildings, places and streets, and how these are connected.

b They are all non-residential buildings or commercial premises.

c near to, on, in, by, across, beyond, behind, next to, between, along, opposite, in front of, alongside, before, after, at, off, past

Questions 6–10: Labelling a map

Key

6 petrol station: The route has been established with the description *when you come out of there* (the bus station) *you turn right* and go *along Orchard Road*. It is *next to the car dealers*.

7 shopping centre: The speaker says the *car park* is at the *first left: Newfield Avenue*, which runs *alongside the shopping centre*.

8 insurance offices: She says by *continuing along Orchard Road*, the *water company* and then *the insurance offices* are *on your right*.

9 hotel: She mentions the *advertising agency* and, *facing* it, *Cherry Lane*. The *newspaper office* is *on the corner*, so the building *opposite* must be the *hotel*.

10 call centre: She points out that their location is Almond Drive, not Cherry Lane, and says *turn right at the next junction*, at the *mail centre*. The call centre (*InterCard*) is *the third building on the right*, between the *airline offices* and the *shipping company* (not shown).

Recording script

Questions 6–10

Ellen:	Can you get over there for 9.45 on Monday morning, for an interview?
Steve:	Definitely, yes. Whereabouts are they?
Ellen:	In Riverside Business Park. Do you know it?
Steve:	Yes, I've been there once.
Ellen:	How do you usually travel?
Steve:	By bus.
Ellen:	Right. So you take either the 136 or 137 to the bus station, and when you come out of there you turn right.
Steve:	Along Orchard Road, that is? The road from the railway station?
Ellen:	Yes, that's right. You go past the **petrol station** next to the car dealers, then carry on down the road.
Steve:	Do I take the first left? At the main car park?
Ellen:	Well you could do that, and walk up Newfield Avenue alongside the **shopping centre**, but it's a long way round. I'd suggest continuing along Orchard Road, with the water company and then the **insurance offices** on your right. They used to be local government offices, by the way.
Steve:	Yes, I remember those.
Ellen:	And you keep going until you reach the advertising agency. Now facing that is a small road called Cherry Lane. There's a newspaper office on the corner and opposite that is **a big hotel**, so you can't miss it.
Steve:	And how far down that road is it?
Ellen:	Well they aren't actually in Cherry Lane. You walk as far as the next junction and turn right into Almond Drive, at the mail centre. **InterCard** is in the third building on the right, between the airline offices and the shipping company.
Steve:	Fine. I'll be there on Monday. Thanks very much. Bye.
Ellen:	Good luck. Bye.

Exploration

4 Possible answers

a patience, general communication skills

Speaking page 64

Aims – Students listen to people describing their occupations and learn useful language for Speaking Part 1.

Orientation

2 Key

speaker a: 2
speaker b: 1
speaker c: 3

Recording script

Speaker a:	My name's Mark Davies and my job is to find out what's going on and report it. The best thing about it is the excitement. I never know what story I'll be covering next, and no two days are ever the same. The only thing I don't like about it are the unsocial hours: if a major story breaks, I have to be there at any time of day or night. My ambition is to be a foreign correspondent with one of the big radio networks.
Speaker b:	I'm Jennifer Symons. I did an MBA at university and nowadays I'm in charge of twelve people selling mainly to manufacturing companies in the area. I particularly enjoy the responsibility and the good salary, but one drawback of working here is that there are limited prospects for further promotion. In the medium or long term my aim is to work for a larger organization, possibly in a different industry.
Speaker c:	My name's Chris Dean and for five months I've been working in the coastal waters off Antarctica, studying a species of algae. What makes the job so fascinating is that every day we're building knowledge, knowledge about how the entire world's ecosystems work. To me the downside to it is not the cold, I'm used to that, but the darkness in the winter months. When this job ends I'll be looking for a permanent position in a marine biology department.

Describing an occupation

3 Key

When checking the students answers, draw attention to the expressions the speakers use to introduce their answers. Point out that these will be useful in Speaking Part 1.

a Mark
   Their responsibilities: *my job is to find out what's going on and report it.*
   What they like about the job: *the best thing about it is the excitement.*
   What they dislike about the job: *the only thing I don't like about it is the unsocial hours.*
   Their future career plans: *my ambition is to be a foreign correspondent.*

b Jennifer
   Their responsibilities: *I'm in charge of twelve people selling to companies.*
   What they like about the job: *I particularly enjoy the responsibility and good salary.*
   What they dislike about the job: *one drawback of here is that there are limited prospects.*
   Their future career plans: *My aim is to work for a larger organization.*

c Chris
   Their responsibilities: *I've been studying algae in waters off Antarctica.*
   What they like about the job: *What makes it so fascinating is that we're building knowledge.*
   What they dislike about the job: *the downside to it is the darkness in winter.*
   Their future career plans: *When this job ends I'll be looking for a permanent position in a marine biology department.*

IELTS practice
Part 1: Familiar discussion

4 Remind students to give full answers, including reasons for the statements that they make. If possible, they should try to use phrases that the speakers used to add details and justifications.

Language for writing page 65

Aims – Students revise comparative and superlative forms which will be particularly useful for Writing Part 1.

Comparative and superlative forms

1 Key

a Their marketing department is much bigger **than** ours.
b Williams is the **best** manager we've ever had.
c Prices have increased **more** slowly this year than last year.

d These are the **worst** figures in the firm's history.
e Family-run firms are sometimes the **most successful** of all.
f Colin works **less** hard than anyone else in this office.
g Production didn't go up any **faster** last month than the month before.

2 Key

a more / less intense   d the greatest
b wider   e worse
c harder   f the most efficient / the least efficient

3 Key

small: slightly, a bit, marginally
large: far, a great deal, significantly
used with superlatives: easily

4 Note that references to spring, summer and autumn refer to the northern hemisphere seasons.

Possible answers

a by far the lowest
b a great deal more quickly
c far the biggest
d slightly higher / a bit higher
e a bit more slowly / a great deal more slowly
f a great deal further / significantly further
   The index was a great deal higher at the end of the year than the beginning.
   The index was significantly lower in the autumn than it had been in the summer.
   During the autumn and winter, easily the highest point was reached in December.

5 Possible answers

a IBM is not (quite) as valuable as Microsoft.
b Toyota is half as valuable as GE. / GE is worth twice as much as Toyota.
c Disney is half as valuable as IBM. / IBM is worth twice as much as Disney.
d Marlboro is as valuable as Toyota. / Toyota is worth as much as Marlboro.
e GE is worth twice as much as Marlboro. / Marlboro is worth half as much as GE.
f McDonald's is just under half as valuable as IBM. / IBM is worth just over twice as much as McDonald's.

Writing page 66

Aims – Students learn to study the information presented in charts and graphs in order to find the links between them. They also practise making comparisons based on graphical information.

Orientation

1 Ask students to work in pairs.

Possible answers

a Internet, newspapers
b newspapers, TV, radio, direct mail
c magazines, TV, newspapers
d newspapers, TV
e radio, TV, magazines
f radio, (local) newspapers

2 Make sure students read the Note before they complete the exercise.

Key

a The pie chart is used to show expenditure in billions of dollars and therefore proportion of spending on each form of advertising in 2005. The bar chart is used to show percentage changes during 2006.
b The proportional share of the advertising market by each media outlet.
TV, direct mail, and newspapers dominate the market.
c The variation in expenditure on each media outlet in 2006.
The overall trend is upwards.

Comparing data

3 Possible answers

a Of all the advertising media, the smallest sum of money was spent on the Internet.
The largest proportion of total spending went on TV advertising.
Direct mail accounted for the next largest amount of total spending.
The lowest projected rise was forecast for radio advertising.
By far the highest expected growth was forecast for Internet advertising.
Increases in the region of 5–10% were forecast for TV, direct mail, newspapers, and magazines.
b the Internet

4 Key

a Almost as much money was spent on direct mail as on TV advertising.
b Relatively slow growth was predicted for newspaper advertising in comparison with magazines.
c Much more was spent on advertising in newspapers and magazines taken together than any other category.
d Apart from two categories, most forms of advertising were forecast to rise by 5–10%.
e Not as much was spent on radio, magazines and the Internet combined as on TV, direct mail or newspapers.

f Internet advertising was expected to increase over twice as much as any other category.

Think, plan, write

5 Possible answers

a By stating accurately what the data shows.
b While spending on Internet advertising was the lowest in 2005, it had the highest projected rise. Although TV, direct mail, and newspapers formed by far the largest proportion of total advertising in 2005, they were expected to grow relatively slowly in 2006.
c TV, direct mail, and newspaper in the first chart; Internet in the second chart. These are the largest segments or show the greatest change respectively.
d The first chart, showing expenditure in 2005.
e TV, direct mail, newspaper, radio and magazines are all expected to show fairly similar increases.
f past simple, future in the past (*was expected, was predicted*)

7 Check students' evaluations to ensure that their feedback is fair and accurate.

Help yourself page 68

The final page in each unit is intended to raise a variety of extra areas that students can explore and to encourage responsibility for their own language learning.

Word formation

1 Key

anti- = opposed to, against, the opposite of
antisocial = not wanting to spend time with other people
anticlimax = something that is a disappointment, not as exciting as you expected

bio- = connected with living things or human life
biodiversity = existence of a large number of different plants and animals
biodegradable = something that can be broken down by the action of bacteria

dis- = negative, opposite of
dishonest = not honest
disobey = refuse to obey

extra- = 1 very, more than usual 2 outside or beyond
extraordinary = unusual, more than ordinary
extraterrestrial = noun: a creature that comes from another planet (not Earth), adjective: connected with life beyond Earth

mis- = bad(ly) or wrong(ly)
misbehaviour = bad behaviour
mismanage = to manage badly

re- = back or again
rewind = to wind backwards (e.g. an audio cassette)
refuel = to fill a vehicle with fuel

2 Key

auto- = of or by yourself / by itself, without a person being involved
Examples: autobiography, automatic, autopilot
inter- = between / from one to the other
Examples: international, interaction, interdependent, intermarry
multi- = more than one, many
Examples: multistorey, multicoloured, multinational, multimillionaire
over- = 1 more than usual, too much
Examples: overcooked, overconfident, overexcited
2 upper, outer
Examples: overcoat, overgarment
3 over, above
Examples: overcast, overhang, overhead
post- = after
Examples: postgraduate, post-war, postdate
trans- = 1 cross, beyond
Examples: transatlantic, transcontinental
2 into another place or state
Examples: transplant, transmission
under- = 1 not enough
Examples: undercook, underdone, undercharge
2 lower in age or status
Examples: undergraduate, underclass, underdog
3 below, beneath
Examples: undergrowth, underground, underpass

3 Key

a employ (verb)
  employee (noun – person)
  employment (noun)
b create (verb)
  creator (noun – person)
  creative (adjective)
c weak (adjective)
  weakness (noun)
  weaken (verb)
d child (noun)
  childish (adjective)
  childhood (noun)
e solid (adjective)
  solidify (verb)
  solidly (adverb)

4 Key

a dehumidifier = a device for taking moisture out of the atmosphere / making it less humid. The root word is *humid* = wet / full of moisture

enclosed = surrounded by, closed in by. The root word is *closed* = shut
undesired = not desired / wanted. The root word is *desire* = want
b multidimensional = with many dimensions. The root is *dimension* = measurement (width, length, height, etc)
outpatient = patient who visits but does not stay in hospital. The root word is *patient* = someone receiving medical treatment.
abusers = people who uses something in a wrong or harmful way. The root word is *abuse* (verb) = to use something improperly.
c increasingly = more and more. The root word is *increase* = to grow / become greater in number.
imperfections = aspects of a person's character which are not perfect, weaknesses. The root word is *perfect* = without fault.

5 Key

right-handed / cold-hearted = adjective + past participle
Other examples: left-handed, warm-hearted, bare-headed, wrong-footed
quick-thinking = adjective or adverb + present participle
Other examples: slow-moving, sweet-talking
a database / the generation gap = noun + noun
Other examples: lamp post, container lorry
an eye-witness account = compound noun + noun
Other examples: chequebook journalism
an outbreak / a downpour = preposition + verb
Other examples: input, output, off-cut
a break out = verb + preposition
Other examples: fall-out, break-through
a blackbird / grandparents = adjective + noun
Other examples: greenhouse, whiteboard
writing paper, driving test, walking boots = present participle + noun
Other examples: gardening gloves, sleeping bag, washing machine

IELTS to do list

Encourage the students to tick one of the boxes and plan to do this task outside class.

Where to look

Students can use these practical tips to find further information.

6 Education

Introduction page 69

Issues – This section introduces the overall theme of the unit, and contrasts the main stages of education.

Aims – Students are given opportunities to compare the different stages of education, and discuss some key educational issues.

1 Ask students to work in pairs or groups to discuss the photos.

Possible answers

Photo 1 shows university eductation. Students go to lectures or study in smaller seminar groups, do lengthy assignments, and get degrees. They usually study a single subject. Universities usually try to foster independent learning.

Photo 2 shows a secondary school, the last phase of compulsory education in most countries. Classes are often large, and teaching for the older children tends to be focused on passing of exams. Children specialize as they get older. There may be behaviour problems, e.g. unmotivated children or bullying.

Photo 3 shows a primary school class. These are smaller schools for children between the ages of approximately 5 and 11. School is usually more fun at this age, with plenty of opportunity for play and creativity. A wide variety of subjects are taught. Children are usually keen to learn because of their natural curiosity.

2 Check that students know the meaning of *lagging behind* (developing more slowly), *faith schools* (schools which follow the teachings and principles of a particular religion) and *truancy* (staying away from school without permission).

Possible answers

a Testing and its effects on the motivation of students.
   Who should pay for higher education. / Financial hardship suffered by students in higher education.
   The gender divide, especially in reading and writing.
   The place of religion in schools.
   How to deal with bullying in schools.

The problem of truancy.
Lack of childcare facilities for working mothers.
Parental choice in education.
Technology in the classroom.

Extra activity

Tell students to choose two or three of the issues they identified in exercise 2c and write a headline for each of them. Remind them of the key features of newspaper headlines – (most) articles are omitted; they must be short and should convey a strong message.

Reading page 70

Issues – This section introduces the issue of gender differences in education.

Aims – Students practise scanning for specific information and identifying opinions, and learn how to apply these skills in matching tasks.

Orientation

1 Ask students to work in pairs or groups.

Possible answers

a The boys are carrying out a manual construction task which involves practical problem-solving. The girls are reading a book which involves concentration and language skills. The boys seem to be all working separately on their own individual models, while the girls are working very closely together even though it is an activity which could be carried out individually.

b There is probably considerable variation in different parts of the world, but in some cultures the following pattern has traditionally been observed: boys tend to be better at science and maths, while girls tend to be better at languages, reading and writing.

c There are two main arguments. Some people believe that boys and girls are innately different in a way which makes them respond differently to different subjects. Others believe that the differences between them are the result of upbringing, parental expectations, the effects of role models, social pressures, prejudice, and so on.

2 Key

a gender gap = the difference between the genders, male and female

literacy = the ability to read and write

an age-appropriate level = a level (of ability) that one would expect at a particular age

Scanning

3 Key

a, b
> Cecilia Reynolds, academic
> Paul Cappon, Director General of the Council of Ministers of Education (politician)
> Leonard Sax, family doctor and psychologist

Identifying opinions

4 Key

a She says we should not assign blame when thinking about differences between boys and girls. However, she admits that insufficient attention may have been paid to boys' learning needs.
Verbs and phrases introducing her opinions: ... *has warned that it is important to address...*, *she does admit* ...

b The kinds of reading materials available in schools may be better suited to girls than boys because boys prefer factual and instructional material, while girls like stories that explore interpersonal relationships.
Phrases suggesting others share his views: *the current wisdom is* ...

c Genetic differences between boys and girls make it impossible for them both to learn in the same classroom. Such differences are that girls hear better than boys and that boys like confrontational teaching, but girls don't.
Verbs and phrases suggesting he believes in the case he's making: *believes that* ..., *He argues ... that* ..., *He claims that* ..., *He also points to* ...

IELTS practice
Questions 1–5: Matching

Key

1 A. Cecilia Reynolds points out that *gender differences are statistical, with significant numbers of individuals everywhere not following the general trend* (lines 107–110).

2 C. Sax argues that there are *genetic differences between boys and girls* ... (line 90–91)

3 A. According to Cecilia Reynolds ... *boys were still going on to get better jobs and salaries* (line 8–9).

4 C. Sax points to research that *shows key differences in the way boys and girls respond to confrontation. Girls shrink away from a confrontational teaching style under which many boys would thrive* (lines 99–103).

5 B. *Increasingly teaching is becoming dominated by females ... That leaves boys with few male role models in the classroom* according to Paul Cappon (lines 54–58).

Questions 6–9: Sentence completion

Key

6 (almost) disappeared (line 20)
7 dropping (each year) (line 29)
8 interpersonal relationships (line 68)
9 absenteeism (line 81)

Exploration

5 Possible answer

b The politically correct notion is that boys and girls are essentially equal in abilities, and to suggest otherwise is sexist.

6 Key

a a gap in the market = a situation where there is a demand from the public which is not matched by supply

b the generation gap = the differences of opinion, lifestyle, etc. between older and younger generations of people (e.g. parents and children)

c a credibility gap = a lack of trust or belief, here created by experience

d a gap year = a year's break from education, usually taken at the end of secondary school; young people often use a gap year to go travelling or do voluntary work

7 Key

The prefix *out-* in *out-perform* means more than.
To outstay your welcome means to stay somewhere even when you are not welcome or wanted.

Possible answers

a Now that they have six children, the family has outgrown the house they've lived in for years.

b I can't get my old computer repaired. I think it has outlived it's usefulness.

c With a brilliant speech, the president completely outmanoeuvred his political enemies.

d Female graduates outnumber male graduates in languages by six to one.

e In our case the advantages of buying a new car easily outweigh the disadvantages.

8 Key

a presenteeism = being at work when you shouldn't be, often because of illness

b to increase by three times = to treble
to increase by four times = to quadruple

9 Key

academic background	labour market
concrete evidence	political correctness
equal opportunity	university graduate

10 Key

a equal opportunity
b concrete evidence
c political correctness
d university graduate
e academic background
f labour market

Extra activity

Have a class debate on the following topic: *Boys and girls should be educated separately to maximize their academic potential.* Choose two speakers to speak in favour of the motion and two to speak against the motion. Give them five minutes to make notes and prepare their speech. Each speaker should talk for a maximum of two minutes. Other students should listen and can ask questions at the end of each speech. At the end the full class votes on the motion to decide whether or not it is carried.

Listening page 74

Aims – Students practise predicting answers to short-answer questions and sentence completion tasks.

Orientation

1 Key

Photo 1: gliding
Photo 2: ju-jitsu
Photo 3: DJ

2 Possible answers

c People often join societies to make friends, to develop an interest or try a new hobby, to get experience which may help with a future career, to experience an activity which may be expensive or difficult to arrange independently.

Predicting answers

3 Possible answers

a sports, drama, film, computer, music, languages, etc.
b 1 a number, e.g. over twenty
   2 a description, e.g. a climbing club
   3 an expression of frequency, e.g. once a week, twice every month
   4 a month or season, e.g. in July
   5 a type of dancing, e.g. salsa

6 an event, e.g. a lecture
7 a place, e.g. the university
8 a place
9 a place
10 a qualification, e.g. grade VIII music
c 8 and 9

IELTS practice
Questions 1–6: Short-answer questions

Key

1 over a / one hundred	4 during the vacation
2 a music club	5 Scottish dancing
3 twice a week	6 a film evening

Recording script

Questions 1–6

Presenter: Hi and welcome to the Students' Union. You've all been here a week now, and hopefully, you're finding your feet. You might be wondering what there is to do on campus apart from going to lectures, doing essays, going out with friends and having late nights. Tonight you're going to hear about some of the societies, clubs, and associations that you can join as a new student, as well as the cultural events going on that might interest you. Richard Hillman, from Student Services has come along this evening to tell you more.

Richard: Good evening – it's good to be here and to see you all. Let me say straightaway that, as students of the university, you are entitled to join, free of charge **over a hundred societies** on the official list. OK, let's begin. I'd be prepared to bet that whatever your interests, you're almost sure to find a club or society here for you. Not surprisingly, there are the long-established clubs that you can find at any university, like the Football Club or the Drama Society, along with a whole range of less usual clubs, for example the Rock Society. We do have a Rock Climbing Club here, **but the Rock Society has nothing to do with outdoor activities – it's a music club.** That takes me neatly on to **the Mountaineering Club.** Now it might surprise you that a university in one of the flattest parts of the country has a thriving group of mountaineers. **They meet twice a week:** on Tuesdays from five in the afternoon until ten o'clock in the evening, and on Thursday afternoons from one o'clock until five.

At their regular meetings they use the climbing wall, but **they also organize trips to real mountains both here and abroad during the vacation**. Another rather out-of-the-ordinary society you might like to try is the Dance Club. They meet regularly every Friday. This term they're running salsa classes, next term it's tango and **in the summer it'll be Scottish dancing** – quite a selection. They also put on special events twice a term – either performances by visiting groups, or actual dances. Their next event is next Saturday when they're putting on a Latin evening. Go along and try out your samba. At the moment the Dance Club is trying to attract new members who may have new ideas for future classes and events. If you're an overseas student you may find there's a society for students from your country putting on events that'll make you feel more at home. The Mexican Society, for example is putting on a special Christmas celebration with traditional Mexican food and drink. And **every four weeks, the Hellenic Society has a film evening**. There are also national societies for Malaysian, Turkish and Chinese students. And don't forget these societies are open to everyone – whether you're from that country or not.

Questions 7–10: Sentence completion

Key

7 Lakeside Theatre
8 the University Gallery
9 the Workshop Studio
10 an audition

Recording script

Questions 7–10

Richard: Finally, I'd like to say something about the **flourishing arts scene here. This is centred mainly on the Lakeside Theatre** and includes a full programme of music, theatre and visual arts. As far as visual arts are concerned, **the University Gallery** has exhibitions throughout the year. The work of local, national, and international artists is regularly on display as well as exhibitions featuring contemporary architects and designers. **The University also has a permanent collection of Modern Eastern European art on display**. As well as the conventional theatre productions, put on by visiting professional companies and student groups, **there is a Workshop Studio which stages more experimental drama**. And finally music. Concerts catering for a variety of musical tastes include performances by visiting groups as well as home-grown talent: the university has its own jazz band and choir. As with the other groups I referred to earlier, you are eligible to join these, but of course **you will be required to go for an audition**. So there you have it. Obviously, I haven't covered everything in this short introduction, but I hope I've given you a flavour of what's on offer here.

Exploration

4 Key

a Normal facilities may include lecture halls, science labs, classrooms, libraries, administration buildings, student accommodation, sports facilities, shops, restaurants, bars, theatres, galleries.
b It is successful.
c He's just *putting* it *on* – He's pretending.
   She had to *put* the brakes *on* = She had to apply the brakes.
   I'd *put* money *on* him = I'd bet / risk money on him.

Speaking page 76

Aims – Students learn the importance of giving personal responses to the tasks in Speaking Part 2 and practise the language of personal reactions.

Orientation

1 Check that students know the meaning of *implementation* (making something happen), *implications* (the possible results of an action or decision), *rational* (based on reason rather than emotions), *analytical* (using a logical method of thought) and *subjective* (based on your own ideas and thoughts rather than facts).

Personal reactions

3 **Possible answers**

My favourite teacher at school was Mrs Roberts, my sixth-form history teacher. My main reason for choosing her is that she was really good at describing the atmosphere of each period of history we studied.
I never enjoyed art classes. The only explanation I can think of is that the teaching wasn't very good,

because I love painting and drawing now.
The most useful thing I learnt at school was how to
cook. For me, this was fantastic because we had
really good cookery classes, and now I'm actually
thinking of training to become a chef.

IELTS practice
Part 2: Extended speaking

4 Tell students that they are going to practise a
Speaking Part 2 task. Remind them to write about
each point listed, using notes and not full
sentences.

5 Students work in pairs. Ask them to time each other
if possible and make a note of how long their
partner spoke for.

Language for writing page 77

Aims – Students revise the use of *-ing* forms and
infinitives.

-ing forms and infinitives

1 Key

a basing, findings, recordings
b to store, giving, to study, (to) analyse
c understanding
d collaborating
e studying, gathering
f to give
g improve
h to get, graduating
i to go, high-achieving

2 Key

a, b after certain verbs: infinitive (Sentences b, h and
     i – *allow us to store, go on to get, want their children
     to go*) and *-ing* (Sentence e – *spend a year
     studying*)
     as nouns: *-ing* (Sentence a – *findings, recordings*)
     to show purpose: infinitive (Sentences b and f –
     giving us time to study, to give children)
     in participle clauses: *-ing* (Sentences a and b –
     Basing, giving us time)
     part of continuous tense: *-ing* (Sentence d – *were
     collaborating*)
     as adjectives: *-ing* (Sentence i – *high-achieving*)
     after prepositions: *-ing* (Sentence h – *after
     graduating*)

3 Possible answers

a Subjects were given opportunities to comment
   on the research methods.

b The survey showed that most people tend to
   respond negatively to cold calling.
c A sample of over a thousand people were asked
   to say how they had voted.
d The questionnaire started by asking people their
   date of birth.
e Without this research, it would be impossible to
   understand why some people can spell better
   than others.
f There are many different ways of interpreting the
   statistics.
g The purpose of the project was to investigate the
   cause of the accidents.
h The report highlights the problem of boys' poor
   scores as well as suggesting possible reasons.
i There are many issues to consider when deciding
   where to live.

4 Key

a learning	k developing
b Answering	l learning
c to study	m trying
d learning	n to answer
e (to) conduct	o carry out
f (to) develop	p improve
g help	q start
h to understand	r imagining
i Running	s explain
j learning	t learning

Writing page 78

Aims – Students practise writing different types of
introduction to their compositions.

Orientation

1 Ask students to work in pairs to discuss the
questions.

Possible answers

a Benefits: University life is enjoyable and broadens
   the mind. Graduates will probably get better
   paid, more satisfying jobs.
   Disadvantages: There is a lot of hard work.
   Where fees are not paid by the government,
   students may end up owing a lot of money.
b If a country has a high proportion of university-
   educated people, there will be a plentiful supply
   of well-qualified people to fill important posts in
   business (which is good for the economy),
   government and administration, and other key
   professions such as doctors, teachers, etc. This
   saves having to recruit and train people from
   other countries.

2 Key

Speaker 1: University students
Speaker 2: Politicians
Speaker 3: Parents
Speaker 4: University authorities

Recording script

Speaker 1: As far as I'm concerned going to university is a two-edged sword. Sure, it's interesting and enjoyable – I've made loads of new friends and hopefully I'll get a useful qualification and a good job at the end of it. On the other hand, I'll have a huge debt to pay back. I've heard people say it can take years for fees and loans to be repaid. So, I'm really enjoying my course, but I must admit I'm a bit worried about what happens afterwards.

Speaker 2: If we want to compete with other countries, we really do need to have at least 50% of our young people in higher education. Especially in areas like technology, science and business, we need young people who are educated to a world class standard. The only way for this to happen is for us to increase access to higher education; this means we have to provide more places at more institutions and therefore extra funding, massive extra funding if we are serious about enabling half or more of our young people to go to university.

Speaker 3: Of course we want what's best for them. When I was that age only about 10% of 18-year-olds went on to higher education. You were special if you went to university in those days – a sort of elite. Now, anyone can go – and I suppose that's a good thing, as long as the universities aren't lowering their standards. Our main worry is money. We think university education should be free for everyone who's good enough to get in. As it is, our son will be paying off his debts for at least ten years. That doesn't seem fair, given that his having a degree will help the country.

Speaker 4: We're all in favour of opening up higher education to as many young people as possible. But of course this costs money – not just in the education itself, staffing and so on, but in additional administrative costs, extra student accommodation. And of course the money's got to come from somewhere. If the government's not prepared to fund us, then we have to depend on other sources. At the moment, our main source of income is home student fees, but in the future we expect to recruit more overseas students who pay higher fees.

Introductions

3 Key

a Fact: Increasing numbers of young people go to university, students will probably earn higher than average salaries.
Opinion: Students (not the state) should pay for their own higher education.

b Students (not the state) should pay for their own higher education.

4 Key

1 against
2 puts both sides of the argument
3 in favour

5 Key

a 1 The idea that ... seems at first glance a fair suggestion
 2 The view that ... is gaining popularity
 3 It is often assumed that ...

b 1 Nevertheless, it makes the assumption that ...
 2 Although I have some sympathy with this idea, ...
 3 However, ..., the assumption that ... is being called into question.

c 1 As I shall argue, this ...
 2 I shall go on to suggest that ...
 3 there are good arguments for ...

6 Possible answers

1 The idea that the purpose of education is to prepare people for work seems at first glance a fair suggestion. Nevertheless, it makes the assumption that finding a good job is people's principal motivation in adult life. There are good arguments for a broader education that can improve our understanding and help us live more fulfilling lives. (argues against)

2 It is often assumed that everybody should have the same basic education. Although I have some sympathy with this idea, many people require little knowledge of subjects such as science and mathematics in everyday life. As I shall argue, these people should be encouraged to find work and get more practical training. (argues in favour)

Help yourself page 80

The final page in each unit is intended to raise a variety of extra areas that students can explore and to encourage responsibility for their own language learning.

Thinking skills

2 Key

The man had put sugar in the original cup of coffee. Because his replacement coffee was sweet, he knew that it wasn't a completely fresh cup.

4 Possible answers

a   Sally. He likes words which have double consonants in them (carrots, apples, lorries and Joanna).
b   If the statement is true, then it must be false; but if it is false then it must be true. The word for such a statement is a *paradox*.
c   The two babies are two of a set of triplets.
d   Both are false. All dogs *are* mammals, but there is nothing in the previous sentences to indicate that this is so.
    It does not necessarily follow that this person was a criminal. It may be that other people, apart from criminals, go to prison.

5 Key

The exercises on this page encourage students to think in a variety of ways. Students practise thinking logically and laterally. To tackle them students should brainstorm (think up) and jot down all the points that come into their heads when considering a particular issue or problem. These thinking skills can be of particular use to students working on Writing tasks 1 and 2 and may be of some value in Speaking part 3. True / false / not given questions in the Reading Module also require students to compare a statement with a section of text and decide whether it agrees with the information in the text, contradicts the information or if there is no information on it in the text.
In multiple-choice questions it is necessary to compare a statement with a section of text to see whether they convey the same meaning. Sometimes an answer option may contain a statement which is true, but does not reflect the content of the text.

IELTS to do list

Encourage the students to tick one of the boxes and plan to do this task outside class.

Where to look

Students can use these practical tips to find further information.

7 Science

Introduction page 81

Issues – This section introduces the overall theme of the unit, covering a wide range of general science questions.

Aims – Students are given opportunities to think and speak about broad scientific issues, learning relevant vocabulary along the way.

1 Check that students know the meaning of *the solar system* (all the planets that move around the sun), *intact* (complete and not damaged) and *helium* (a light colourless gas, sometimes used to fill balloons).

Key

a False. The Olympus Mons on Mars, at 24 km in height, is three times as tall as Everest.

b True. Carbon dioxide is heavier than air, so it stays on top of the burning material, thus preventing oxygen reaching it.

c True. The water in the balloon, unlike air, will completely absorb the heat of the flame.

d False. They are filled with nitrogen, an inert gas which does not corrode the metal used in aeroplane tyres. It is virtually non-combustible.

e False. The heat exchanger at the back of the fridge will heat up the room more than it cools the inside of the fridge, as it takes more energy to cool something down than warm it up.

f True. There is generally more life in cold, moving waters, partly because cold water has a higher oxygen content.

g False. Each whole number on the Richter Scale represents a 32-fold increase in energy, so an 8 is 32 x 32 times stronger than a 6. The correct answer is therefore 1,024 times stronger.

h True. Light travelling at very high speed towards the eye is perceived by the brain as being blue. Conversely, if it is moving away very fast it will appear to be red. This is one example of the *Doppler effect*.

2 Key

a astronomy, geology
b physics, chemistry
c physics
d chemistry
e physics
f biology, chemistry
g geology
h physics, astronomy, biology

Reading page 82

Issues – This section introduces the topic of astronomy, and focuses on the efforts of scientists to build an array of giant telescopes to observe distant galaxies.

Aims – Students learn to identify different description schemes, and practise reading a text quickly for gist.

Orientation

1 b

Recording script

The simplest reflecting telescope, developed by Newton in the seventeenth century, consists of a wide tube pointing at the sky with a large, concave mirror at the bottom. Light rays from space travel down the tube and strike this primary mirror. The light is reflected upwards to a much smaller 'secondary mirror' in the centre of the tube. The secondary mirror is set at an angle of 45°, so the light is then reflected out to the left-hand side where it can be viewed through a round eyepiece lens at 90° to the tube.

Description schemes

2 Key

a Time: after that, a few seconds later
b Spatial: a little further down, going anti-clockwise, from left to right
c General to the specific: overall, taken as a whole
d Importance: even more difficult, by far the biggest
e Topical: the third item, another part

3 Key

a The first sentence is general to specific. It then becomes spatial as it follows the path of the light rays.

b the contents of a library: spatial
a firm's management structure: importance
a hurricane: time and spatial
a home cinema system: topical, spatial or general to specific
an animal's appearance: general to specific
a chemical process: time
a space rocket: general to specific, spatial and / or time

Reading for gist

4 Key

a A series of giant telescopes, known as the Atacama Large Millimetre Array.
b In the Atacama desert, Chile.
c To observe microwave radiation from distant galaxies.

5 Key

Paragraph C.
It is first general to specific to ... *recorded and analysed* (line 28). It then becomes spatial as it describes the position of the parts.
Words: outwards, down, on, beneath, on.

IELTS practice
Questions 1–4: Labelling a diagram

Make sure students read the Note before they complete the task.

Key

1 dish (line 24)
2 sub-reflector (line 26)
3 rotating structure (line 31)
4 (steel) base (line 32)

Questions 5–11: Multiple-answer questions

Key

5–7 (in any order)

B. The text says there are *no trees, no bushes, not even a blade of grass* (lines 3–4).
C. It goes on to say that oxygen levels are puny (lines 5–6).
E. The writer describes the rainfall as *negligible* (line 9).
It cannot be A as it refers to *rolling featureless hills* (line 2). The temperature is not mentioned nor are any local people, therefore D and F are not correct.

8–9 (in any order)

A. The writer states that the receivers are *transportable* (line 23), and refers to an adjustable grid of tracks (line 34).
D. The text mentions that *putting together such a mammoth piece of kit* in the Andes will be *outrageously ambitious* (lines 36–39).
B is not correct because the 6,000 square metres mentioned in the text refers to the size of the collecting surface (line 36) not the land covered. The mention of a football pitch (line 36) again refers to the collecting surface not a real pitch, so C is incorrect.
E is incorrect because the text doesn't mention who is paying for it.

10–11 (in any order)

C. The writer states that scientists *still need to learn about its early infancy thirteen billion years ago,* (lines 49–50) and then describes the changes that were taking place then.
E. The text says that because microwave radiation is absorbed by water an observatory at sea level would *pick up nothing* (lines 70–71). But Chajnantor, which is high and dry, *is perfect for picking up microwaves* (line 75).
It cannot be A because astronomers know what the earth was like ten billion years ago (line 47). The text also says scientists *are now satisfied they know about the universe's birth* (line 49) so it cannot be B. The telescopes at Chajnantor are located and designed to take into account the Doppler shift not to minimize it so D is not correct.

Questions 12–14: True / False / Not given

Key

12 True. *An observatory at sea level would pick up nothing* (lines 70–71).
13 True. *That is why we picked Chajnantor. It is high and dry – perfect for picking up microwaves* (line 74–75).
14 True. *... mankind has been exploiting the aridity of the Atacama desert for millennia. This is the place where mummification ... began* (lines 75–77).

Exploration

6 Key

featureless – empty
arid – desiccated
dead – lifeless
negligible – puny
hostile – inhospitable

7 Key

a giant, vast, mammoth
b faint
c fluid

d cosmos, heavens
e human beings
f collecting, picking up

8 Possible answers

a featureless, empty, inhospitable, hostile, arid, desiccated, vast
b inhospitable, hostile, giant, vast, mammoth
c inhospitable, hostile
d featureless, empty, lifeless, inhospitable, vast
e featureless, vast
f lifeless, inhospitable, bright

Listening page 86

Issues – This section introduces the topic of ethical standards in science.

Aims – Students discuss some of the ethical issues relating to science before practising multiple-choice and multiple-answer questions on this topic.

Orientation

1 Key

a The use of pesticides which may include damaging chemicals.
Medical interference in the reproductive process.
The picture shows IVF, or in vitro fertilization, which may allow otherwise infertile couples to have babies.
The dangers of nuclear power, specifically exposure to nuclear radiation.

Possible answers

d It is vitally important that scientists maintain ethical standards otherwise it is possible for scientific research to be used in a way that is damaging to society.
e It would be very beneficial if science courses trained students in ethics, as this would help to promote greater ethical awareness amongst scientists.

2 Key

A tutorial, probably at a university.
The history of modern science. / Ethics in science.

IELTS practice

Questions 1 and 2: Multiple-choice questions

Key

1 C. The tutor gives examples of *the benefits* and *terrible damage* brought about by science. A is false, as she says *the relationship between scientists and society became much closer* in the twentieth century. She then says they *became increasingly concerned about the ethics of what they were doing*, so B is also false.

2 B. The student says *they ought to stop making any distinction between pure science and applied science.* He talks of the *duty* of scientists to *make public the findings of their research* and adds *they need to do that*, so A is false. He also states that *they must accept full responsibility for the consequences of their work*, so C is false.

Recording script

Questions 1 and 2

Carol: In the nineteenth century, scientific discoveries took a long time to produce any actual applications, and scientists might have had a case for giving little thought to the social or environmental impact of their work. That all changed in the twentieth century, with the huge advances first in physics and then in biology. Science started to play a much more important role in our lives, and the relationship between scientists and society became much closer. Many scientists became increasingly concerned about the ethics of what they were doing as they quickly saw the consequences: **the benefits** such as vastly improved crop yields and the eradication of diseases like bubonic plague, **but also terrible damage** in the form of pollution and chemical weapons.

Matt: Yes, but some scientists still claim, even today, that their only duty is to make public the findings of their research. They need to do that of course, but I think the key points are that **they ought to stop making any distinction between pure science and applied science** because in practical terms it no longer exists, and also they must accept full responsibility for the consequences of their work.

Questions 3–10: Multiple-answer questions

Key

3–5 (in any order)

B. This answer is suggested by *advise on what might one day go wrong as a result of what they're coming up with now.*

C. This answer is found in the statement *if and when things do go wrong they need to sort things out.*

F. This is covered in the statements about *the way the public sees scientists* and the need to *work on* this, to *regain public trust.*

A is not correct because although one student says scientists can put responsibility into practice by educating the public, there is no suggestion that this needs improving only that it needs to happen. The possibility of discoveries going abroad is not mentioned. Therefore D is not correct. E is not correct because the female student says *I'm not suggesting getting involved with politics or politicians.*

6–8 (in any order)

A. This answer is suggested by *adding specific genes to plants.*

C. Evidence for this is found in the statements *using chemicals to control pests* and *spraying of crops.*

F. This is covered in the references to *death on a massive scale* and *chemical and biological and nuclear warfare, which has destroyed life.*

B and D are not mentioned. There is a reference to the environmental damage aircraft cause but it is not specifically linked to changing weather patterns. Therefore E is also not correct.

9–10 (in any order)

B. The tutor refers to scientists who take planes to distant places *too often* and goes on to say it damages the environment.

D. She mentions *the huge distances a lot of consumer goods travel before they actually reach the shops in this country* and says this is an extreme waste of energy. Car journeys and wasting energy in our personal lives are mentioned by the male student not the tutor so A and E are not correct. The tutor talks about the use of video conferencing as a way that computers can benefit the environment, so C is not correct.

Recording script

Questions 3–10

Carol: Let's explore that last point a little further. How can scientists put that responsibility into practice?

Matt: By educating the public, particularly through the media and at the workplace.

Jan: Another thing they must do is **advise on what might one day go wrong as a result of what they're coming up with now**.

Matt: That seems essential. And just as importantly, **if and when things do go wrong, they need to sort them out**, especially where the fault lies with the original research.

Carol: How do you feel about the international role of scientists, given that their work crosses frontiers so readily?

Jan: I think it gives them, or at least should give them, a global view. In this respect some of them are better placed than many politicians to see how new discoveries are likely to affect particular parts of the world.

Matt: But will the politicians listen?

Jan: Probably not, but I'm not suggesting getting involved with politics or politicians. Much better to raise the public's awareness of scientific issues, so they can put the pressure on at election time.

Matt: There's a problem here, though, isn't there, with **the way the public sees scientists**: they're all either mad or bad.

Jan: That's **something they need to work on**, definitely. **To regain public trust** they'll have to show they're accountable, and that science is about improving people's lives.

Carol: That may not be so easy. What do you think are the areas in science that really worry people these days?

Matt: Science in agriculture, above all. There's been all this media hysteria about 'Frankenstein Foods' but there is a genuine issue here: whether **adding specific genes to plants** is a valid way of increasing food production, or whether it risks the appearance of new diseases, of super-weeds and pests.

Jan: Which links it to another controversy: **using chemicals to control pests**. And that's something else that was at first thought to be harmless, but we now know that the careless **spraying of crops** has led to all kinds of health problems for people. Plus a devastating loss of biodiversity, with huge numbers of insects, birds and mammals simply disappearing from the countryside, fish dying in poisoned rivers, and so on.

Matt: And of course if we're talking about **death on a massive scale**, then we have to mention the role of science in enabling the military to wage **chemical and biological and nuclear warfare,**

which has destroyed life in so many parts of the world.

Carol: OK, I think we've identified some major topics there.

Matt: There's something I'd like to add, if I may. Sure, it's important for scientists and future scientists to talk about major issues like these, but we might also want to look at what we can do or not do in our everyday lives, particularly as many of us will be earning more money than we actually need for basic necessities. I'm thinking here of things like burning fossil fuels by driving everywhere. What do you think?

Carol: Well **something that scientists seem to do rather too often is take planes to distant places**, which is highly damaging environmentally.

Matt: For instance to attend conferences on subjects like the disappearing ozone layer ...

Jan: When nowadays they could probably stay at work and use a video conferencing link anyway ...

Carol: Which may in fact be an example of how progress in computer science can impact positively on the environment.

Matt: But going back to harmful things. What else can be done?

Carol: Again on the air transport theme, there are **the huge distances a lot of consumer goods travel before they actually reach the shops in this country.** This seems another extreme waste of energy, especially if much of what is being produced and carried is packaging. Perhaps it's worth shopping for more locally-produced items?

Exploration

3 Possible answers

b We can do this by buying fair trade goods and avoiding buying products which are illegally sourced or connected with animal cruelty, e.g. ivory, animal shells, fur, and certain cosmetics. In addition we can avoid products produced in sweat-shops. We can also question whether we need certain products or whether we could do without them.

Speaking page 88

Issues – This section introduces a number of moral issues related to current scientific discoveries.

Aims – Students learn to develop their opinions and extend their answers by analysing the advantages and disadvantages behind different issues.

Advantages and disadvantages

1 Possible answers

B BENEFITS: extremely complex calculations could be carried out by computer; computers may be able to 'think' for themselves
DRAWBACKS: it might be difficult to control these computers; they may be potentially dangerous in the 'wrong' hands
MORAL ISSUES: these computers will be extremely powerful, but would be unable to make moral judgements
UNEXPECTED CONSEQUENCES: computers could start to control humans, e.g. a computer could become head of state, or could start a revolution

C BENEFITS: a longer life would appeal to many people
DRAWBACKS: these extra years might involve a great deal of ill health
MORAL ISSUES: interference with the natural processes of the human body
UNEXPECTED CONSEQUENCES: health services and pension systems would collapse due to an ageing population

D BENEFITS: loss of life and damage to buildings could be vastly reduced
DRAWBACKS: countries without access to this technology could suffer, especially if hurricanes are diverted towards them
MORAL ISSUES: the danger of upsetting broader weather patterns
UNEXPECTED CONSEQUENCES: this could be developed into a new military weapon

E BENEFITS: women could have greater choice over when to give birth, e.g. they could follow their career before having children
DRAWBACKS: older mothers may experience

difficulties during pregnancy and labour, and
may be less able to look after young children
MORAL ISSUES: many people would see this as
an unnatural interference with the workings of
nature
UNEXPECTED CONSEQUENCES: it could lead
to the cloning of human beings

IELTS practice
Part 3: Topic discussion

2 Make sure students read the Note before they
complete the task.

Language for writing page 89

Aims – Students revise passive forms, which may be
particularly useful for Writing Task 1.

Passive forms

1 Key

a The process is repeated.
b The process is not repeated.
c It is formed with *be* + past participle.
d Because it's obvious or unknown, or we prefer
not to say. It is common to omit the agent when
describing processes.
e The passive is common in: academic writing and
describing processes, to focus on actions and
situations more than the people responsible for
them; formal letters for greater impersonality;
newspaper headlines (in reduced form) to save
space.
f Intransitive verbs, because they do not take an
object, e.g. *happen, fall*. Certain common verbs
such as *let* and *get*. The passive is rarely used with
the future continuous (*be being*) or future perfect
continuous (*been being*).

2 Key

a Past simple. A sample of the compound was
placed in a tube.
b Present perfect. The tube has now been placed in
hot oil, with a thermometer.
c Future simple. The melting temperature of the
sample will be noted.
d Present simple. The purity of the sample is
shown by the temperature.

3 Key

Sentence b is passive.
The new information is the use of a specially-
designed pump.

4 Key

a This vapour is then cooled by an unusually-
shaped condenser.
b Following the printing stage, the letters are
delivered by bicycle couriers.
c Now that it has gone through six phases, the
process will be completed by a final test.
d These small particles of dust are attracted by an
electrically-charged object like a TV screen.
e Once the refining procedure was over, colouring
was added to the product by certain
manufacturers.

5 Key

The power of the Earth's air pressure is shown by
the following simple experiment. First, a large
container is filled with cold water. Next, 15 ml of
water is poured into an empty Coke can. The can is
held in kitchen tongs, heated and allowed to boil
for approximately thirty seconds. When the can is
full of steam, it is removed it from the heat and
partly immersed, upside-down, in the cold water. It
collapses immediately as the steam condenses,
creating a partial vacuum. The can has been
crushed by the difference between the external and
internal air pressure.

Writing page 90

Aims – Students learn sequencing expressions and
study the language of processes before putting
these into practice in a Writing Task 1.

Orientation

1 Key

a photosynthesis
b rice
c sugar cane
d two thousand times
e cactus
f Australia

2 Key

The process shown is that of taking a cutting from
a plant to grow a new one.

Sequencing

3 Key

1 f 2 d 3 a 4 b 5 c 6 e

4 Key

d **Firstly**, a sharp knife is used to cut away a non-
flowering shoot from the body of the plant.
a **The next step is to** remove the lower leaves of the
shoot so that only one or two pairs of leaves
remain.

b **Then**, the bottom centimetre of the cutting is dipped in rooting powder.
e **Finally**, the cutting is placed in a pot containing soil and watered thoroughly.

5 Key

FIRST STAGE: first of all, in the first place
LATER STAGES: secondly, subsequently, after this
SAME STAGES: at the same time, simultaneously, meanwhile, alternatively
FINAL STAGE: in the end, lastly, ultimately

6 Key

Then, a polythene bag is placed over the pot to prevent drying out.
Finally, the pot is placed in a window, shaded from direct sunlight.
Change e to *after this*.

Think, plan, write

7 Key

a The process by which a greenhouse heats up.
b Three
c Present simple passive

Help yourself page 92

The final page in each unit is intended to raise a variety of extra areas that students can explore and to encourage responsibility for their own language learning.

English spelling

1 Each statement represents a different view on English spelling which students may be able to identify with. There is no right answer.

2 Recording script

1 ageing
2 excellent
3 controversial
4 independent
5 necessary
6 beneficial
7 category
8 knowledgeable
9 significance
10 commitment
11 controlled
12 exaggerate
13 successful
14 maintenance
15 attendance
16 opportunity
17 recommend
18 analyse (NB: US English – analyze)
19 embarrass
20 fulfil (NB: US English – fulfill)

3 This exercise shows students that there are regularities that they can identify for themselves, although there are also exceptions.

Possible answers

a take —> taking, revise —>revising
b hot —> hotter, dig —> digging
c pretty —> prettier, happy —> happily
d sky —> skies, carry —> carries

4 This exercise shows that apparent irregularities often make sense once you understand the patterns in more detail.

Key

a A final -*e* is not dropped when the word ends in two vowels.
b A final consonant is not doubled: when there are two vowels before the consonant; when there are already two consonants at the end of the word; when there are more than two syllables in the words and the final one is not stressed.
c A final -*y* is not changed to -*i*: when the ending starts with -*i* (-*ing*); when there is a vowel before the -*y*.

IELTS to do list

Encourage the students to tick one of the boxes and plan to do this task outside class.

Where to look

Students can use these practical tips to find further information.

8 IT and communications

Introduction page 93

Issues – This section introduces the overall theme of the unit, focusing on recent developments in IT and communications.

Aims – Students are given opportunities to think and speak about the impact of new technologies.

1 Ask students to work in pairs to discuss the photos.

Key

Photo 1: iPod
Photo 2: digital photography
Photo 3: online banking
Photo 4: satellite navigation systems
Photo 5: bluetooth

2 Ask students to work in groups to discuss questions a and b.

Possible answers

b Health: Many areas of health treatment – including transplants, keyhole surgery and reproductive health – have undergone major changes due to technological advances. Some of these technologies – such as facial transplants, and stem cell research – have raised ethical concerns.
Relationships: New technology such as mobile phones and email have made it much easier to keep in touch with people, but in some cases 'virtual relationships' become a substitute for real face-to-face contact.
Crime: Genetic fingerprinting has led to increased crime detection and fewer miscarriages of justice. However, there are concerns about invasion of privacy and possible abuse of power if governments were to keep mandatory records of genetic fingerprints.
Trust: Online shopping has provided consumers with a vastly increased access to a huge range of local and international goods. However, this system of shopping relies heavily on consumer confidence. Buyers need to be able to trust that purchasing systems are secure and that they are not exposed to credit card fraud.
Addiction: Online gambling, including card games like poker, has become an extremely popular leisure activity in many countries. This has lead to an increase in addiction problems.
Politics: Electronic voting has created the potential for a much quicker and more reliable counting of votes, but there are concerns that such a system may be vulnerable to hacking and other corrupt practices.

d Many people dislike change, so they instinctively prefer older, familiar technologies. New technology can be difficult to understand, especially for older people.

Extra activity

Students work in pairs or groups. Tell them that they are going to invent a new form of technology. Give them some examples (a car that drives itself, an automatic system that orders food supplies as soon as they run out, a self-cleaning room). Write the following headings on the board: *How does it work? Who are the main customers? What are the advantages and disadvantages?* Students work together to think of ideas and one member of each group writes a short description. Students read their descriptions to the class.

Reading page 94

Issues – This section introduces the topic of wireless technology, and its affect on working practices.

Aims – Students practise making notes, and study the layout of tables such as those that they will find in table completion tasks.

Orientation

1 Key

a A system of sending and receiving signals without the need for wires.
A radio. It includes mobile phones, Bluetooth GPRS and WiFi.
c It allows people to contact each other, or a computer network, from any location, including when on the move.
d Communicating or working from a fixed base, i.e. an office or home, with telephone landlines and a fixed computer network.

Making notes

3 Make sure students read the Note before they complete the task.

Key

Para 1
Key idea   three technologies associated with mobile working
Details   mobile phones, text messaging and **email**
Para 2
Key idea   **advantages** of mobile devices for **employees**
Details   lets them work **on the move**; there is less **wasted time**
Para 3
Key idea   real-time working
Details   benefits to **businesses**, employees and **customers / clients**
Para 4
Key idea   **Flexibility** of mobile devices
Details   advantages and **disadvantages** of this **flexibility**

4 Possible answers

Paragraph 5: Bluetooth technology – the advantages and disadvantages
Paragraph 6: WiFi techology including the need for 'hotspots' – the advantages and disadvantages
Paragraph 7: GPRS – the advantages and disadvantages
Paragraph 8: Security and cost – a comparison between the three technologies
Paragraph 9: The future of wireless technology – manufacturers want to push ahead but users will decide

5 Make sure students read the Note and refer them to the example table which follows.

Key

a The three technologies are compared by range, data transfer speed, cost, and who they are best suited for.
b Information needed:
   Range: distance measurement in metres(?) / kilometres(?)
   Data transfer: a number in MB
   Cost: amount of money – in sterling(?) / in dollars(?)
   Best for: a type of activity
c The organization of the table allows easy access to factual information. It also facilitates the classification of information which may be buried in a dense prose text.

IELTS practice

Questions 1–7: Table completion

Key

1 10 metres (line 54)
2 100 metres (line 70)
3 54 MB (line 64)
4 £50 (line 91)
5 £40–£60 (line 95)
6 travelling (line 67)
7 reliable communication (line 76)

Question 8: Multiple-choice question

Key

8 B. The text looks at different forms of wireless technology. It includes a brief history the advantages and disadvantages and where it may go in the future. A is not a good title as it is the opposite of the main idea in the final paragraph, which says it it the *users, not the developers of technology who will finally decide which ideas take off.* C is not accurate because the text does not make direct comparisons between wired and wireless technologies. D is wrong because the impact of wireless technology on productivity is one small part of the content of the text.

Exploration

7 Key

Singular verbs are used in these sentences because the subject is a singular noun: *a new generation* (a), *a range* (b).

8 Key

Plural verbs are used in these sentences because in the case of a the subject is *The advantages,* which is plural (*workforce* identifies which advantages but is not the subject). In the case of b *staff* – like *workforce* – is a collective noun which can be thought of as a number of individuals and can be singular or plural. Words in the same category: audience, class, club, committee, company, congregation, council, crew, crowd, family, gang, government, group, jury, team

9 Key

a is / are
b has
c meets / meet
d presents
e has
f is
g has

10 Key

a provide	e download
b edited	f place
c access	g transmit
d update	

Listening page 98

Issues – This section introduces the topic of the Internet as a source of reliable information.

Aims – Students learn to analyse and understand flow charts like the ones they may encounter in the Listening paper. They also practise a summary completion.

Orientation

1 Possible answers

a Advantages: It provides access to millions of pages of information. It is the largest single source of information available, and the most up-to-date source of information. It is accessible to all and much information is free. It is quick and easy to access from any computer.
Disadvantages: It's not always easy to find out where to look. Search engines also control the order of the websites they inform you of. Furthermore, much information is unreliable, it can take a long time to find relevant information. A lot of material is commercial and biased in some way. The information is not always updated, and there's a lot of rubbish cluttering the Internet.

c Recent research: academic journals, possibly the Internet
Yesterday's national news: a newspaper, the Internet
Information about a rock band: the Internet, a music magazine
Historical information or biography: a library, the Internet

Understanding flow charts

2 Key

a The flow chart represents a sequence of actions. The boxes on the left side (Step A–Step E) are stages in this sequence, with the arrows showing the progression from one step to the next. The boxes on the right side list the actions that have to be taken at each step.

b The structure suggests that the information will be about the stages of a process which involves a particular sequence of actions involving changes to text.

c abbreviated, note form, sequencing vocabulary

d Finally: Step 5
Let's start by: Step 1
It is at this point that: between Step 2 and Step 4
The first step: Step 1
When this has been done: any time after Step 1

IELTS practice
Questions 1–2: Short-answer questions

Key

1 an encyclopedia
2 unpaid volunteers

Questions 3–6: Flow-chart completion

Make sure students read the Note before they complete the task.

Key

3 input	5 preview (option)
4 summarize	6 (click on) save

Questions 7–10: Summary completion

Make sure students read the Note before they complete the task.

Key

7 accuracy	9 vandalism
8 reputations	10 neutrality

Recording script

Jenny: Good afternoon. I'm Jenny Ironbridge and today I'm going be continuing my series of talks on information technology, by looking at an innovative information source available on the Internet. I'm sure you're all familiar with the strengths and weaknesses of the popular search engines like Google or Yahoo. Sometimes you can find what you're looking for instantly. At other times searching for something which may or may not exist can be a frustrating and time-consuming experience. So, where can you go to get the information you want? The information source I want to talk about is called **Wikipedia**. As its name suggests **it's a form of encyclopedia**. It's already the largest information source in history both in terms of its breadth and its depth. But what makes Wikipedia really unique is that it's a democratic project. The content is completely free to access, and **it's written entirely by unpaid volunteers**. Changes and additions are being made all the time to articles which exist already, but it's also possible to contribute whole new articles. And basically, **anyone can contribute, once they've grasped the basics of editing the pages**.

Let's look at how someone goes about editing Wikipedia articles. It's a very straightforward procedure which has been made deliberately easy so that people who have contributions to make are not discouraged from participating because of their limited understanding of information technology. Let's start by imagining that we are reading an article and we come across information that we consider to be incorrect or incomplete on a page of Wikipedia. First of all, we decide we'd like to change it. To do this, we click on the Edit button at the top of the page. This takes us to another page with a text box containing all the editable text on that page. It's at this point that we can **input** our changes in exactly the same way as we would if we were writing or editing a document we had created on our own computer. In other words, we can type, cut and paste, delete and use all the normal word-processing functions. When this has been done and we've finished editing, we are then asked to **summarize** the changes we have made. This doesn't go into the main text box but into a separate area below it. That's the main part of the process over with, but we need to make sure that the changes we've made are going to appear as we want them. A last check, if you like. In order to do this we select the **preview option**. If we're still not satisfied, we have the option of returning to the edit stage and working through the same procedure again. Finally, if we're satisfied with the result, we simply **click on save**, and our changes will take immediate effect.

A question that might already be forming in your mind if you are not familiar with Wikipedia is this: **'How can I tell whether information is accurate?' This particular point has led to criticism from some people, especially academics and professionals.** The short answer is that you can't tell, but, if you think about it, how can you check the accuracy of information you read in a conventional encyclopedia, or in a newspaper or on other Internet websites. **Besides, it's possible for contributors to Wikipedia to register with the organization, and,**

as named contributors gradually build up a reputation for themselves as reliable sources of information. The other point to be aware of is that there are administrators who monitor contributions that are added by anonymous sources and check for biased, out of date, or incorrect information. **One of the problems that arises from the openness of Wikipedia is that vandals have gone into the site to change and damage pages of information, so the administrators have a role in policing this too.** Lastly, Wikipedia encourages editors to stick to certain rules, which help ensure the quality of entries. **For example, contributors are expected to maintain a neutral tone in their writing, although perhaps it's impossible to be completely neutral.** Also, entries are not allowed to include original research, which is intended to prevent contributors from simply submitting their own views. It's unlikely that the more conventional information sources will ever be completely replaced by Wikipedia or similar projects which may be developed in the future, but this is an ambitious experiment to democratize information, using modern technology to enable anyone and everyone to contribute to and access a common body of knowledge. And because it's free, it doesn't restrict access to those with the ability to pay.

Exploration

3 Possible answers

b Commercial reference sources, both conventional (books, encyclopedias, magazines, etc.) and online reference sources which require subscriptions. Secret organizations, governments or corporations who do not want their secrets revealed to the world.

Speaking page 100

Issues – This section introduces the topic of future developments in information technology and their effects on society.

Aims – Students practise the language of speculating which may be particularly useful for Speaking Part 3.

Orientation

1 Possible answers

b People used to read and write using books, pen and paper, or a typewriter.
People used to play board games, play phyical games or do sport.
People used to listen to music: live, on CDs, cassettes, records, on the radio.

Speculating about the future

2 Key

speaker 1: c
speaker 2: a
speaker 3: b

Recording script

Speaker 1: Hmm, that's a big question. Obviously modern technology makes our lives easier in many ways, and gives us more leisure time than we've ever had, but there are more things to worry about than there were in the past and stress levels are higher than they used to be. I think **this can only get worse**. In fact, **I'd say it's fairly unlikely that** technology itself **will make us happier**. It may make people expect more out of life and then feel disappointed because the reality doesn't live up to their expectations.

Speaker 2: **I think it's quite likely that many more people will work from home in the future.** To some extent this is already happening. I suppose this will probably mean that there'll be less need for large offices in the centre of cities, as more and more employees access their computers from their homes.

Speaker 3: As I see it, **it all depends on** individuals. I don't think that the technology itself will change our behaviour or somehow **stop us wanting to spend time with our friends and other people**. On the other hand, a lot of people seem to want to shut the world out by spending a lot of time listening to music through headphones or playing computer games. **If this continues**, it could result in more people feeling lonely and isolated.

3 The purpose of this activity is to provide a reference list of expressions that students can use when they are asked to speculate about the future.

Key

I think it's quite likely that …
I'd say it's fairly unlikely that …
If this continues, it could …
It all depends on …
This can only get worse.
This will probably mean that …

Language for writing page 101

Aims – Students revise the uses of adverbs and adverbial phrases, which will help to make their writing more interesting and varied.

Adverbs and adverbial phrases

1 Key

a completely / vastly
b conclusively / definitively
c highly / statistically
d rapidly / sharply
e Amazingly / Not surprisingly
f clearly / consistently
   seriously / severely

2 Key

Certainty / Expectation: inevitably, naturally, predictably, (not) surprisingly, obviously, without a doubt, of course, as might be expected, (quite) clearly, undoubtedly
Evaluation / Importance: apparently, disturbingly, unfortunately, fortunately, interestingly, quite rightly, significantly
Generalization: as a general rule, by and large, typically

3 Key

a Not surprisingly, crime rates have risen in line with unemployment figures.
b Fortunately, there is a very satisfactory solution to this problem.
c Apparently, technology will cause more problems than it solves.
d As a general rule / Generally speaking, older people don't adapt so easily to new techonology.
e Interestingly, children often pick up new skills for themselves.

Writing page 102

Issues – This section introduces the possible negative aspects of technological developments.

Aims – Students learn to develop their written opinions with supporting arguments and examples.

Supporting ideas

2 Key

b *What is really important in life* probably refers to the less materialistic side of life, to do with relationships, feelings, creativity, etc.

Possible answers

c Computers, mobile phones, and similar devices allow us to communicate very easily, but sometimes this is a substitute for real, face-to-face contact with others. In the areas of thought and creativity, computers now do many of the things that people used to do for themselves.

3 Possible answers

a People send each other emails or text messages. Consequently, they talk face to face or on the phone less than they used to.

b Some people use the latest gadgets because they convey status rather than because they are a means of increasing communication. This further distances them from the importance of relationships.

c Some people tend to spend a large proportion of their time at the computer – avoiding real contact with other people and missing out on physical and cultural activities.

d Certain skills, such as designing using traditional methods, are no longer needed. Calculators have made mental arithmetic largely redundant.

4 Make sure students read the Note before they complete the exercise.

Key

a The first sentence

b Sentence 2 provides a supporting argument related to the first sentence.
Sentence 3 makes an additional point related to the main argument.
Sentence 4 rounds off the paragraph with a personal comment by the writer.

c 1 A good example of this is (that) / One example of this is (that)
2 In addition to this
3 As might be expected / Disturbingly / Predictably / Not surprisngly / Unfortunately

Think, plan, write

6 Possible answers

a This phrase conveys the idea that although we may think of access to information, etc. as being beneficial, it is in fact the very opposite.

b Children could be at risk of coming across violent and pornographic material. Terrorists might find bomb-making instructions, etc. and use the Internet to communicate with each other and recruit new supporters.

Help yourself page 104

The final page in each unit is intended to raise a variety of extra areas that students can explore and to encourage responsibility for their own language learning.

Using the Internet

1 Each statement represents a different view on the Internet which students may be able to identify with. There is no right answer.

3 Possible answers

a All the items could be useful sources of vocabulary; magazines and newspapers could be particularly good sources of useful expressions related to current issues; pop songs and radio programmes could improve listening skills; reference information could help in improving accuracy.

b Newspapers, radio programmes, online libraries, academic journals and magazines could provide useful topical content on issues that will appear in the exam.

c All the items could provide information in one form or another about English-speaking countries and their cultures.

4 Key

blog: Formed from the expression *web log*, this is a personal site in the form of an online diary for others to read, and / or a place to write opinions on, for example, a social issue.

chat: This allows people to communicate directly with others online. Messages and replies appear on the screen in real time, as they are written.

keypal: This is like a penfriend, but uses the medium of email rather than conventional letters. English could be used as the language of communication or a mixture of English and the writer's first language.

discussion list: There is one for every imaginable
topic. You can read what people have written on
the topic and take part by sending in emails
which others may respond to.

IELTS to do list

Encourage the students to tick one of the boxes and
plan to do this task outside class.

Where to look

Students can use these practical tips to find further
information.

9 Social issues

Introduction page 105

Issues – This section introduces the overall theme of the unit, focusing on a range of different social issues and some possible solutions.

Aims – Students are given opportunities to think and speak about broad social issues, learning relevant vocabulary along the way.

1 Ask students to work in pairs or groups to discuss photos 1–4.

Possible answers

a Photo 1: two parents looking after children. This photo suggests the pressures of time and financial resources there can be on families with young children.
Photo 2: housing. This photo shows high-density, probably low cost, housing, suggesting differences in where and how people live.
Photo 3: education. This photo shows boys in school uniform and suggests the way the school and type of education shape our lives.
Photo 4: consumerism. This photo shows highly packaged and relatively expensive food in a trolley. This represents the change in lifestyle brought about by consumerism and the divide between those who can afford such items and those who cannot.

2 Check that students know the meaning of *racial discrimination* (treating a particular racial group of people in a society unfairly) and *class privilege* (advantages given to a section of society, usually at the upper economic level).

Key

1 d   2 c   3 a   4 b

3 Ask students to work in pairs or groups to discuss questions a–e.

Possible answers

a They should be incorporated into society in a way that involves them and doesn't lead to social problems or dependence on the state.
c They should introduce fair trade policies, i.e. stop subsidizing their own producers, lower trade barriers, insist on paying a proper economic rate for produce.

d Possible measures could include: stricter discrimination laws; positive discrimination (guaranteeing jobs, housing, etc. to ethnic minorities); education programmes.

Reading page 106

Issues – This section introduces the topic of friendship.
Aims – Students learn how to work out the meanings of words by identifying their roots.

Orientation

1 Check that students know the meaning of obligations (things you must do because you feel that you ought to, or it is your moral duty to do them).

Word formation

2 Make sure students read the Note before they complete the exercise.

Key

neighbourhood: root word = neighbour
neighbour → neighbourhood (changes a noun to another noun)
inclusion: root word = include
include → inclusion (changes a verb to a noun)
justification: root word = justify
justify → justification (changes a verb to a noun)
usefulness: root word = use
use → useful (changes a verb to an adjective)
useful → usefulness (changes adjective to a noun)
friendliness: root word = friend
friend → friendly (changes a noun to an adjective)
friendly → friendliness (changes an adjective to a noun)
virtuous: root word = virtue
virtue → virtuous (changes a noun to an adjective)
mobility: root word = mobile
mobile → mobility (changes an adjective to a noun)

3 Key

inter- = between
un- = not
in- = not
under- = less, below
counter- = against, in reaction to
in- = not

4 Key

overstatement = exaggeration, a claim that is too strong or positive
unevenly = not evenly, unequally
counterproductive = having the opposite effect of what is intended
intolerance = unwillingness to accept ideas or ways of behaving that are different from your own

5 Key

Friendship is the *invisible thread* because the author regards it as an abstract force which holds society together. *Thread* is another word for cotton, or other material, used to sew clothes to hold them together.

IELTS practice
Questions 1–6: Locating information

Key

1 F. It says *It is now widely acknowledged tha women do more of the 'social' work ... which leaves men at a disadvantage.'* (lines 54–56)
2 A. The text says, *The wondrous good in friendship* (line 3) and further down remarks that *friendship barely gets a mention among academics or policy-makers* (lines 10–11).
3 C. This opens by saying *One of the reasons why thinkers struggle to recognize this trend may be one of definition* (lines 22–23).
4 D. This makes the statement that *There are few numerical limits on the first two kinds* [of friend] ... *but true friendship is ... a limited field* (lines 36–40).
5 G. The writer asserts that *People from a particular social class or background are highly likely to form friendships ... with people from the same background* (lines 59–63).

6 B. This paragraph says that *while the claim that friends are the new family is an overstatement ... friendships figure predominently in both the lives people actually lead and the ones to which they aspire* (lines 14–18).

Questions 7–13: Yes / No / Not given

Key

7 No: He says *its significance in our lives is, if anything, increasing* (lines 13–14).
8 Yes: According to the author *true friendship is by definition a limited field* (lines 39–40).
9 Yes: The text says *Virtuous friendship ... brings great psychological benefits, and ... is associated with a range of health benefits* (line 41–42).
10 Not given
11 No: According to the text *political institutions can improve or worsen the conditions in which friendships are fomed* (lines 76–78).
12 No: The author says *Ironically, for politicians to discourage people from working long hours could be counter-productive ...* (lines 86–88)
13 Not given

Exploration

6 Key

self-help books = books which tell people how to do things for themselves
policy-makers = people who make policies, e.g. governments, boards of companies, or other establishment groups
walk-on parts = unimportant roles (a theatre expression used for bit part actors who appear on stage but do not speak)
political downsides = political disadvantages
cross-class friendships = friendships between people from different classes (they have to cross class barriers to become friends)

7 Key

a groan = are full of. Literal meaning: make a low moaning noise because of pressure or pain
b slippery = difficult to pin down. Literal meaning: impossible to hold
c hoard = hold on to for themselves, not share. Literal meaning: keep (not spend) money or other valuables
d erode = undermine, damage. Literal meaning: wear away

Listening page 110

Issues – This section introduces the topic of voluntary work.

Aims – Students practise note completion and short-answer question tasks.

Orientation

1 Ask students to work in pairs or groups to discuss the questions.

Possible answers

a People of all ages might sign up because of feelings of anger at global injustice, sympathy for people worse off than themselves, or a desire to experience other situations.

Young people may in addition have a sense of adventure, a desire to see the world and / or youthful idealism.

Older people, on the other hand, may want a change from their usual career, or have a feeling that they can make use of particular experience or skills they have acquired.

b Governments should ensure that all of the world's people have sufficient resources to live in reasonable comfort. However, in extreme conditions of drought and other natural disasters voluntary aid may be necessary. Alternatives include government aid, international aid and self-help. The former two can help with basic provisions of seeds, tools, etc., and appropriate education, to allow the poor and underprivileged to fend for themselves and, therefore in the longer term, help themselves.

IELTS practice

Questions 1–5: Note completion

Key

1 22
2 Primary Education
3 two years
4 conservation
5 wildlife protection

Recording script

Questions 1–5

Assistant: Hello, Volunteers Worldwide, how can I help you?

Ben: Hello, I'm ringing to find out about opportunities for doing volunteer work. Could you give me some information, please?

Assistant: Yes, certainly – but before I do, I need to ask you for a few personal details – that's just because the opportunities open to you are dependent on your age and on what qualifications and skills you have.

Ben: That's fine.

Assistant: So, if you could just start by telling me your name and age.

Ben: OK, my name's Ben Oppermann and **I'm twenty-two years old**.

Assistant: OK. And what qualifications do you have, Ben?

Ben: I've got a BA degree in Social Studies, that was from the University of Kent. And I'm a qualified teacher. I've just completed my PGCE, my **post-graduate certificate in Primary Education**.

Assistant: And you're interested in doing unpaid voluntary work rather than a full-time job with our organization?

Ben: Yes, that's right. I'd like to do voluntary work before I start looking for a more permanent job.

Assistant: How long were you hoping to work for us for?

Ben: I was thinking of **two years at most**.

Assistant: OK, well for people in your age group, we have two programmes: Global Youth Contact and Youth for Action on Development. GYC – Global Youth Contact – is a six-month exchange programme which provides opportunities for young people from different countries to work together in local communities.

Ben: I see, but that's only a six-month programme?

Assistant: That's right, but our other programme – Youth for Action on Development – requires people to volunteer for a year at least. On this programme most of the placements are for 12 or 18 months.

Ben: That'd be the programme I'd go for.

Assistant: OK. Now, do you have any other skills or special interests that might be useful for the kind of work we do?

Ben: Well, I've done a lot of **conservation work** in the area where I live.

Assistant: Good, that's useful to know.

Ben: And I **belong to a wildlife protection group**.

Assistant: Right, that could be very helpful.

Questions 6–10: Short-answer questions

Key

6 nine months
7 January
8 two thirds
9 one week
10 September

Recording script

Questions 6–10

Assistant: Do you have any questions you'd like to ask me?

Ben: Yes, could you tell me what sort of placements are available?

Assistant: Well, all our placements are related to the four main areas that we work in, that's: Education, Health, Social participation, and Employment.

Ben: Education sounds like the obvious choice for me. And if I wanted to go ahead and apply to work on a programme like this, what do I have to do?

Assistant: OK, well our **selection procedure is quite a lengthy process**, I'm afraid. **It can take up to nine months**. We get many more applicants than we have placements for, so we need to make sure that we get the best people for the kind of work we do. It's very important to realize that voluntary work like this is not an easy option. Although you'll have a brilliant experience with us, you are expected to work hard and make a real contribution – it is not just sitting around enjoying a different culture.

Ben: Of course, I understand that.

Assistant: OK, so, if you're interested, I can send you an application pack. You complete the forms and send them back to us. **If you are short-listed, we invite you to come for an interview – that's normally in January**. Assuming you are successful, we then start looking for a suitable placement. While we are doing this, we ask you to raise some funds of your own, so that **you end up contributing about two-thirds of the cost of your training and travel**.

Ben: OK fair enough. I suppose people get sponsorship do they?

Assistant: Yes, lots of volunteers do that. Then, in June, we ask you to come to our headquarters for **a week's training**. This starts with general training which is applicable to all volunteers. It includes topics like: how to fit into new cultures; looking after yourself, mentally and physically; and how to go about relating to the kinds of people you'll be working with. And then you'll have sessions related specifically to your placement. We'll tell you about the country and the area you'll be going to, about the problems and difficulties to expect, and about the kind of responsibilities you'll have once you're there.

Ben: And when does the work start?

Assistant: It depends, but **generally speaking, placements start in September** and run for up to eighteen months.

Ben: Sounds brilliant. Could you send me an application pack please?

Assistant: Yes, certainly. If you'd like to give me your address.

Ben: OK. It's 29 …

Exploration

2 Key

dependent: root word = depend
Dependent is an adjective but -*ent* ending could also be a noun.
placement: root word = place
-*ment* is a noun ending. Other examples: government, parliament
contribution: root word = contribute
-*tion* is a noun ending. Other examples: solution, pollution
sponsorship: root word = sponsor
-*ship* is a noun ending. Other examples: championship, sportsmanship
qualification: root word = qualify
-*tion* is a noun ending. See contribution above
applicant: root word = apply
-*ant* is a noun ending sometimes referring to a person. Other examples: defendant, merchant
option: root word = opt
-*tion* is a noun ending. See contribution above
responsibilities: root word = responsible
-*ity / ities* is a noun ending. Other examples include calamity, unity

3 Key

a worldwide = across the entire world
b underprivileged = less privileged than others, than the majority
c irregular = not regular

4 Possible answers

a Education: teaching children, helping in the classroom, producing resources
Health: nursing, being a doctor, feeding and washing patients, giving health advice
Social participation: helping individuals integrate, running clubs and organizations
Employment: helping people apply for jobs or acquire skills

c Voluntary work is very popular, but there is not enough money to fund all those who want to do this kind of work. Some people are not suitable or do not have the necessary qualifications.

Speaking page 112

Issues – This section introduces the topic of cultural identity.

Aims – Students develop their understanding of cultural identity through discussion, and then use diagrams as a way of generating ideas for a presentation. Extensive speaking is useful practice for Speaking Part 2 and will help students in academic study.

Orientation

1 Possible answers

family life: Families provide basic personal identity, cultural heritage, personal history, basic moral values, e.g. concepts of right and wrong, acceptable behaviour, etc.

education: This teaches cultural and social values.

the media: In general this reflects national concerns, ideas and interests.

strong traditions: These establish concrete elements of cultural identity which people can readily identify with.

community: This promotes a feeling of belonging to a social group with the same economic interests and aspirations.

festivals: These give a sense of belonging to a cultural or religious heritage

moral and political beliefs. These are more personal but are shaped by cultural norms.

national sporting achievements: Such achievements promote a feeling of pride in national identity.

2 Explain that students needn't draw pictures, only different size circles.

3 Ask students to work in pairs or groups to discuss their diagrams. In a multinational class, you could compare how the diagrams differ with the whole class.

Giving a presentation

5 Make sure students read the Note before they complete the task.

Possible answers

a Ideas could come from:
Your own experience, family and friends, and local news.
Notes can help as reminders of the structure of the presentation and details to include.
Short notes, concentrating on key points, are probably the most helpful as they are easy to read.
In the context of giving a presentation to fellow students informal language is appropriate.

b You should begin by defining the topic, with an interesting example, or with a question to listeners.
Use written notes as prompts rather than as something to be read out. They will prevent you drying up.
If you dry up refer to notes and repeat previous idea by using different words, or ask a question.

Language for writing page 113

Aims – Students revise features of collocation.

Collocation

1 Key

1 dealing with   3 make
2 prevailing   4 highly

2 Key

Definition b is correct.

3 Key

a present findings, carry out a survey
b make an assumption, a fundamental assumption, formulate a strategy, a long-term strategy
c raise a question, a serious question, basic rights
d international standards, heavy industry, highly efficient
e put forward an argument, a convincing argument, make a case, a strong case for
f The general public, accept the fact, fundamentally distinct, distinct view, views on a subject

4 Key

a question   c raise
b make   d give

5 Key

a serious   c simple
b strong   d possible

Extra activity

Ask students to choose three of the collocations from exercise 4 and three from exercise 5 and write a sentence for each which illustrates their meanings.

Writing page 114

Issues – This section introduces the topic of the family as a support network.

Aims – Students learn to recognize the main features of academic language and use them in their own writing.

Orientation

1 Possible answers

a The picture shows different stages of growing up. The view it portrays is fairly neutral, although the scenes of family groups holding hands are quite positive. However, the child in the main image looks a little anxious, so this could be considered to be a negative image.

b Parents help children with most of their practical and emotional needs for the years while they are growing to adulthood; grandparents can also offer support at this stage. In addition, siblings can help each other by sharing knowledge and skills. Parents may help adult children financially, for example with college fees or when buying a house. Children can help their parents as they get older, perhaps providing financial help or a secure environment to live in.

Academic style

3 Key

2 a   3 b   4 a   5 a   6 b

4 Key

Impersonal style: 2a (it is often argued...)
Formal vocabulary: 1b (decreasing, young people, parents)
Choice of correct terms: 4a (relatives)
Correct use of collocation: 6b (face the daunting prospect)
Correct use of linking words: 3b (However, ...)
Longer complex sentences: 5a (..., whereas ...)

5 Possible answers

Large extended families are also *beneficial for older people* as they become more dependent on others. *Furthermore,* having more helpers available means that the caring can be shared. In smaller families, *senior relatives* may have to rely on a single carer or public resources.
Having a *close relative* in a particular career can also provide useful links and practical assistance for younger relatives who *desire to follow* the same path. *In conclusion it can be stated that* being part of a large family group provides a lot of benefits, *such as* the support that other family members can offer.

Help yourself page 116

The final page in each unit is intended to raise a variety of extra areas that students can explore and to encourage responsibility for their own language learning.

Giving presentations

1 Key

a Presentations are given in the following situations: by students, when presenting a piece of work or study to other students; when a commercial product is first introduced to the public; as part of an in-company training programme.

c It is similar to a presentation in that students have to make themselves clear to their audience. It is not a chat but an expression of opinion supported by examples. It is unlike a presentation in that students are given only a very short time in which to prepare what they are going to say (one minute) and there is limited opportunity to make written notes. Students are given the topic they have to talk about. They have no choice and therefore it is not an extension of their work. The 'audience', in this case the oral examiner, cannot be actively involved whereas in a normal presentation they could.

2 Key

a Talk 1: A lecture, perhaps at a conference or on a university course. The speaker is a lecturer and an academic.
Talk 2: A classroom, perhaps in a secondary school. The speaker is a teacher.

b Talk 1 is much more formal, containing fairly complex sentences and advanced or technical vocabulary. It refers to academic sources.
Talk 2 is more informal and conversational, including several direct questions to the audience. The language is more direct and straightforward.

Possible answer

c The primary purpose of Talk 1 is to convey information in a clear and interesting way. This is effectively achieved, as the speaker puts the information across clearly and sets out the content of the lecture which is to follow. The purpose of Talk 2 is also to inform the students, and perhaps in a classroom situation there is even more of a necessity to make the topic interesting. This is not effectively achieved, because the teacher does not allow the students to present their own ideas.

Recording script

Talk 1

Speaker: Today I shall be looking at what we mean by the term 'community' and the importance of the concept of community from a sociological point of view. In everyday life, the term community has a wide range of meanings. It can be applied to places, for example the village community, to social groups like the student community, to religious or racial groups, like the Buddhist community. Even among sociologists, there is little agreement about a precise definition, although there is a degree of acceptance for Newby's broad ideas. Newby defined 'community' in three main ways: firstly as a social system, that is a set of social relationships; secondly as a fixed locality, in other words a geographical location; and thirdly a quality of relationship, by which he meant a spirit of community. Some sociologists regard these three aspects of community as interlinked, but Newby insists that they are distinct. Newby illustrates his point by pointing out that we cannot guarantee that living in the same locality automatically promotes a warm spirit of community.

Talk two

Speaker: Today we'll be looking at what we mean by the term 'community', and I'd like to start by asking you to tell the student sitting next to you what different communities you belong to. When you've done that, go on to think of a definition of 'community'. I'll give you a couple of minutes for that.
OK, let's find out what you came up with. How many of you said a community was essentially a geographical location, maybe somewhere people live – a village, for example?
OK, thank you. And how many preferred to describe a community as a group of people with similar ideas – like a political party for example?
Thank you. And, finally, how many thought of community as something less tangible, a feeling of belonging, perhaps, an emotional location, if you like?
OK. Well that's very interesting

3 Possible answers

Tip 1: Equipment
  Practise using any equipment or aparatus beforehand.
Tip 2: Planning
  Write headings and brief notes that you can understand at a glance.
Tip 3: Practising
  Practise referring to written notes while you speak.
  Practise using your voice effectively. Don't speak too quickly or too slowly. Vary the pitch and volume of your voice.
Tip 4: Starting
  Break the ice with a joke or anecdote related to your topic. Involve your audience in some way, for example, by asking them a question.
Tip 5: Rounding off
  Summarize the key points you have made in your presentation.

IELTS to do list

Encourage the students to tick one of the boxes and plan to do this task outside class.

Where to look

Students can use these practical tips to find further information.

10 The natural world

Introduction page 117

Issues – This section introduces the theme of wild animals and their effect on humans.

Aims – Students are given opportunities to read and speak about different animals and to discuss their impact on humans.

1 Key

harmless: basking shark (Photo 2)
can injure but not kill: platypus (Photo 1), centipede (Photo 5)
sometimes kills: blue-ringed octopus (Photo 3), crocodile (Photo 6)
kills the most people: mosquito (Photo 4)

2 Key

a Photo 6
b Photo 3
c Photo 2
d Photo 5
e Photo 4
f Photo 1

3 Possible answers

shark: because some sharks are extremely dangerous, because of the portrayal of sharks in films and media reports, and because of our natural disadvantages in water.
crocodile: because they are very large and fierce looking, because of media reports about attacks on humans, and because of our natural disadvantages in water.
Other creatures: spiders, snakes, bears, large cats such as tigers and lions.

4 Ask students to work in pairs or groups to discuss questions a–c.

Possible answers

b They were possibly told originally to encourage children to be careful around dangerous creatures and not to stray away from home. They are told now because we have a fascination for things that are dangerous and unexplained.
c Animals are often portrayed as having very human qualities, and even as being capable of making moral judgements. This may lead people to stereotype species into good (e.g. rabbit, deer, dog, elephant) and bad (e.g. wolves, snakes, hyenas and crocodiles).

Reading page 118

Issues – This section introduces a deadly animal, the box jellyfish.

Aims – Students learn to summarize paragraphs, in order to answer matching heading tasks, and practise different ways of guessing at unfamiliar vocabulary.

Orientation

1 Key

a a jellyfish
b its sting, its eyes

Possible answers

c tentacles, body
d tentacles for stinging and disabling prey, body for digesting prey

Paragraph summaries

2 Possible answers

Paragraph A: Chris Slough gets stung while swimming in the sea.
Paragraph B: Sting caused by an irukandji jellyfish, one of the most toxic creatures on earth.
Paragraph C: Box jellyfish are a mystery.
Paragraph D: Box jellyfish are numerous, but not real jellyfish.
Paragraph E: Box jellyfish are voracious predators who can control their movement.
Paragraph F: Box jellyfish have complex visual systems for seeking out prey.
Paragraph G: Their lethal toxin is to kill prey.
Paragraph H: Chris Slough suffered a lot of pain, but survived.

IELTS practice
Questions 1–7: Matching headings

Key

1 Paragraph B: ix *Irukandjis ... grow no bigger than a peanut, yet relative to their size are probably the most toxic creatures on earth* (lines 18–22).
2 Paragraph c: vii *In fact, almost everything about box jellyfish is a mystery* (lines 39–41).

3 Paragraph D: vi *What the biologists are finding comes as a big surprise* (lines 54–56).

4 Paragraph E: i *Jamie Seymour ... has developed a technique for tracking chironex's movements* (lines 66–79).

5 Paragraph F: viii *They have twenty-four eyes, arranged in clusters of six, one on each side of their cuboid body* (lines 86–89).

6 Paragraph G: ii *It's one thing to stalk fish, but how do you catch them them when all you have are flimsy, rubbery tentacles? The answer is to take them out with as much lethal force as possible* (lines 116–120).

7 Paragraph H: iv *And he was lucky to have a short bout — it only took twenty hours for him to stop feelng like he was going to die* (lines 140–148).

Unfamiliar vocabulary

3 Make sure students read the Note before they complete the exercise.

Key

a You don't need to understand them. They are descriptive adjectives. The nouns following them provide meaning.

b discharge: verb (can be a noun); flat: adverb (can be a noun); rattled: adjective (can be a verb)

c anchored: root word anchor = part of boat; nauseous: root word nausea = feeling sick; light-sensing: root words light = rays from sun, and sense = able to detect

d stings: This also appears as *sting, stung*, and *stinger*. It conveys the idea of poisoning via the skin.
tentacle: Further references in paragraphs C and G give an indication of the appearance of the tentacles and suggest part of the body linked to stinging.
species: The uses in paragraphs B and D indicate the meaning *kinds*.

e toxic: synonym venomous (line 29) = transmitting poison; invisible: synonym transparent (line 25) = can't be seen; primitive: opposite sophisticated (line 110) = highly refined or developed.

f Pre-Cambrian: The text provides an explanation: *543 million years ago* (line 59); cursory: The use of the word *even* shows that the nature of the survey is limited.; corneas: This is part of a listed lexical set with *lenses* and *retinas* (line 99), which are parts of the human eye.

4 Key

mild = not severe or strong. The line below (line 31) indicates it is the opposite of *powerful*.
venom = poison. The meaning can be reached from its repetition in other contexts
painkillers = drugs to reduce pain. This is formed from *pain* and *kill*

characterized = described the qualities of. The next line (line 38) contains the synonym *identified the properties of*.

dim-witted = not intelligent. This is formed from *dim* (not bright) and *wit* (intelligence).

tag = place a tracking device on something. This is followed by *one of these* (line 74), which refers back to *ultrasonic transmitter* (line 70).

underlies = is the basis of or cause of. This is formed from *lie* and *under*.

voracious = greedy, wanting large amounts of food. This is provided in the context that they have *whole chunks of fish inside them* (lines 80–81).

predators = an animal that kills and eats other animals. The meaning can be found from the fact they are in search of their opposite, *prey* (line 84).

drifting around aimlessly = moving along on the current, without control over direction. Meaning can be assertained from the fact that as predators they don't do this but *charge around in search of prey* (line 84).

confined to = kept within certain limits. The text refers to the fact that they were thought to be confined to certain areas but in fact are not, and that *irukandjis too are probably widespread* (lines 132–133).

IELTS practice
Questions 8–11: Sentence completion

Make sure students read the Note before they complete the task.

Key

Logically impossible combinations:

8 A, B, E	10 A, D, E, G
9 A, B, D, F	11 A, D, F

Answers

8 D because they cause much less pain than the venom. The text says *The sting itself is often so mild that you barely notice it until the powerful venom kicks in.* (lines 30–31)

9 G because the exact nature of the venom is unknown. Paragraph C says *no one has characterized its venom.* (lines 37–38)

10 F because they need to go after the fish they eat. We are told *they charge around in search of prey.* (line 84)

11 B because these creatures live in more places than was realized. The text says that *chironex fleckeri was thought to be confined to northern Australian waters but has now been found in Papua New Guinea ... and Vietnam.* (lines 127–132)

Questions 12–14: Short-answer questions

Key

12 543 million years (line 59)
13 tiny ultrasonic transmitters (line 70)
14 a brain (line 99)

Exploration

5 Key

kick in = starts to act. Clues are in words *barely notice* [the sting] *until* (lines 30–31).

brush up against = touch lightly. The clue is in Chris feeling only *a couple of little stings* but thought nothing of it suggesting there was no grip (lines 4–6).

stick on = attach with glue. The clue is in *superglue* (line 71).

head for = move towards. The clues are in the words *immediately* and *straight to the bottom.*

swim off = swim away. The clue is in the information that they covered *half a kilometre* (line 77).

deal with = make sense of, understand. The clues are in the fact it must do something with *information* without having a *brain* (lines 98–99).

send out = transmitting. This can be understood from the words *eyes*, which can produce signals, and *information* (lines 101–102).

seek out = look for and find. The sentence containing *swim around obstacles* and *home in on individual fish* (lines 112–113) gives us the clue. We already know from the previous sentence that this is in the context of hunting.

home in on = aim at a particular target and move straight towards it. We know the fish is hunting from previous information. The word *individual* (line 113) gives us the sense it is hunting something particular.

take out = kill. We are told the context is catching fish. In the context of the previous paragraph (F) the catching is in relation to hunting and killing.

6 Key

a Although Irukandjis grow no bigger than a peanut, they are probably the most toxic creatures on Earth.
b Although Irukandji stings are severe and frequent, no one has characterized its venom.
c Although it can kill a grown man in three minutes flat, no one knows what's in its venom.

Listening page 122

Issues – This section introduces the topic of national parks.
Aims – Students learn to recognize both the written and spoken forms of abbreviations which may well appear in note completion tasks.

Saying figures

1 Make sure students read the Note before they complete the exercise.

2 Key

Thirty-three milligrams
The Nineties
Eight hundred and fifty cc
Three thousand, six hundred and thirty-four square kilometres
Four hundred and fifty five BC
Eight thousand, eight hundred and fifty metres
Fifteen hundred pounds (one thousand, five hundred pounds)
Three point one four one
Five foot ten inches
A hundred miles per hour
Two-thirds
Seven centimetres per day
Thirty-seven degrees Centigrade
Twenty-five squared

3 Key

Area: 1,510 sq km (one thousand, five hundred and ten square kilometres)
Altitude: 1,500–2,180 m (one thousand, five hundred to two thousand, one hundred and eighty metres)
Rainfall: 83 mm / month (eighty-three millimetres per month)
Temperature range: 12–30°C (twelve to thirty degrees Centigrade)
Species: 80 mammals, 450 birds (four hundred and fifty)

4 Key

a Kenya
b The climate is often hot and very dry, with a rainy season.
c Open grassland (savannah) with small clusters of trees.
d Big cats (lions, cheetahs, leopards), elephants, black rhinoceros, giraffes and wildebeest. There are very large numbers of migrating wildebeest; the black rhinoceros are very rare.

6 Key

a The vegetation is much lusher and greener, and so there is presumably much higher rainfall all year round.
b all of them
c 1: square kilometres
3: kilometres /ˈkɪləmiːtəz/
5: degrees centigrade /ˈsentɪɡreɪd/
6: millimetres /ˈmɪlɪmiːtəz/
d 2: hours
4: road number
7: amount of money
8: day and month

IELTS practice
Questions 1–8: Note completion

Key

1	39,000	5	18
2	4 hours	6	2,000
3	280	7	£25
4	A82	8	23 July

Recording script

Questions 1–8

Presenter: Today I have with me Moira Mackenzie, the author of several books in a well-known series of travel guides, and she'll be talking about what is probably the most fascinating wildlife area in Europe: the Scottish Highlands. Moira.

Moira: Yes, that's right, and it's a wonderful place to visit with lots to do in an area that makes up over half of Scotland. Including the seven hundred and ninety islands that lie scattered around the coast, it covers **thirty-nine thousand square kilometres**. Getting there is easy. From here in Glasgow a good starting point is Fort William on the west coast, with regular bus and rail services linking the two. I'd recommend the train, which takes **four hours** to get there. Alternatively, you can take the Highland Line which takes the more easterly route up to Inverness. That in fact is a bit quicker, taking around three and a half hours to cover the **two hundred and eighty kilometres** from here. There are also two main options by road. You can take either the A9 up through Stirling and Perth and then on to Inverness, or else on the west there's the A82, which runs up to Fort William and then, if you want, on to Inverness. Now a lot of people associate the Highlands with bitterly cold weather, but in fact the region has a generally mild climate as a result of being surrounded on three sides by sea, particularly the warm waters of the Atlantic. At sea level in the west, for instance, the temperature ranges on average from a minimum of one degree Centigrade in January up to **eighteen** in July, and you can actually see palm trees growing there. Obviously, though, the temperatures will be lower inland and on higher ground. You can expect it to rain a lot, too, particularly in the west where annually as much as **two thousand millimetres** regularly falls, though this helps account for the rich variety of vegetation and wildlife. When you get there, you'll find there are plenty of reasonably-priced places to stay. In Fort William, for instance, you can find a room for the night in a small hotel or a bed and breakfast for just **twenty-five pounds**, or for twenty-eight to thirty pounds in Inverness. It's probably a good idea to book ahead, though, especially in the summer months. With all the leisure, sports and cultural activities on offer, the towns are becoming increasingly popular with visitors. For example, accommodation in Inverness won't be at all easy to find this year around the **twenty-third of July**, as that's when the local Highland Games will take place. So if your aim is to see the countryside, it may be best to stay in a small village.

Questions 9–10: Multiple-answer questions

Key

C, D (in any order)

C. Moira says *visitors are advised to use their cars if no purpose-built hides are available* and then explains why *people are apparently less likely to startle animals if they stay inside their vehicles*.

D. She says *it's essential to be as quiet as possible*. It is not A because she recommends *avoiding brightly coloured garments such as orange anoraks*. It is not B because she talks about people using hides and staying in vehicles. E is also not correct because she says *wild animals and pets don't mix*.

Recording script

Questions 9–10

Moira: As I mentioned, there's a huge range of wildlife in the Highlands, but for those visiting the area there are some basic ground rules that are essential if we are to protect it. Firstly, you should make every effort not to disturb birds and animals, and one way of doing this is to blend in with your surroundings, for instance by avoiding brightly-coloured garments such as orange anoraks. To see wildlife clearly, it's best to use binoculars, keeping your distance. This is particularly important during the breeding season. Wherever possible, use a hide so that they are less likely to detect your presence. Surprising though it may seem, **visitors are advised to use their cars** where no purpose-built hides are available, as people are apparently less likely to startle animals if they stay inside their vehicles. You may even find that creatures come up close to where you're parked, in which case wait until they've gone before you move off. It should really go without saying that it's essential to **be as quiet as possible**, though sadly some people need reminding of this. Oh, and one other thing: wild animals and pets don't mix, so please leave your dog at home, or at least somewhere he or she can't chase the wildlife or damage their habitat.

Speaking page 124

Issues – This section introduces the topic of animals in zoos.

Aims – Students are given opportunities to consider both sides of an argument, and practise the language of opinions.

Expressing opinions

1 Possible answers

a For:
  To preserve endangered species.
  To allow scientific study of animals.
  To allow people to enjoy animals that they wouldn't otherwise be able to see.
  To provide an unparalleled source of education about the animal kingdom.
  Against:
  It's cruel to take animals out of their natural habitat.
  It's cruel to deprive animals of their freedom and keep them in cramped living conditions.
  The results of research in zoos are unreliable because animals behave differently in captivity.
  It's unfair to use animals for human entertainment.

2 Make sure students read the Note before they complete the exercise.

Extra activity

Write the following question on the board: *What arguments can you think of for and against animal testing for medical or other research?* Students discuss the question in pairs or groups. Remind them to include their own opinions and other people's views. Ask them to read out their opinions and then take a vote amongst the class on whether or not animal testing is justified.

Language for writing page 125

Aims – Students revise clauses of concession which are important in formal academic writing.

Concession

1 Key

1 a Nevertheless
  b Although / Even though
  c despite / in spite of
  d yet / but / although
  e yet / but
  f Despite / In spite of
  g However,
  h Although / Even though

2 Key

a of running quickly, the young deer couldn't escape from the lion.
b there was a minor dip in wale sightings in July, the figures for the year show substantial growth.
c it is not a long snake, the Death Adder is extremely dangerous.
d covering / the fact they cover less than 7% of the land.
e However / Nevertheless, some plants survive there.
f made certain plants less common, but / although sub-tropical varieties have largely replaced them.
g but / yet / although nowadays there are few fish in it.
h five years ago the wolf population stood at just twenty-two, their numbers have risen to over a hundred since then.

3 Possible answers

a Although it seems strange, the butterfly population is actually rising.
b Over a million hectares of wetlands have been lost, yet the destruction continues.
c Even though the rate of extinctions has slowed a little, the total number is still rising.
d Despite the initial fall in panda numbers, the overall trend is upwards.
e They are going to build the motorway in spite of the growing protests.
f Sixty per cent more money was spent, but agricultural production was twenty-five per cent lower.

Writing page 126

Aims – Students study different methods of organizing information, and apply this to a Writing Task 1.

Organizing information

1 Key

a Changes in tiger populations in various Asian countries 1998–2005.

b The change in tiger population levels between 1998 and 2005.

c Populations fell in most countries. However, in Russia the population increased, and populations remained fairly stable in Indonesian and Malaysia.

2 Key

1 Burma
2 Thailand
3 India
4 China
5 Indonesia (or Malaysia)
6 Malaysia (or Indonesia)
7 Russia

3 Key

India remained the country with by far the largest tiger population, **but** experienced a dramatic fall in numbers so that in 2005 there may have been as few as 2000.

Despite its size, China had a very small population of at most 100 tigers by 2005.

Although the trend was downwards overall, tiger populations were thought to have remained stable in Indonesia and Malaysia at approximately 500.

4 Key

b

5 Ask students to work in pairs to discuss these questions. Emphasize that the best approach depends on similarities and differences they spot in the graphs.

Possible answers

A Key points – There has been a relatively steady fall in global populations for animals one and two throughout the period 1905 to 2005. The steepest falls for both animals occurred around 1955–1965. The population of animal three has remained fairly constant throughout the period, although there was a temporary rise in population around 1960 and levels in 2005 were slightly lower than at the beginning of the period in 1905.

Best approach to description – Say what the graph shows. Describe the general trend for animals 1 and 2. Contrast this with the trend for animal 3.

B Key point – Mammals make up nearly 50% of the diet for both animals. Birds form a minor part of the diet of both animals, at less than 10%. Fish are the second largest food source for animal 1, forming a quarter of the diet, with vegetation representing just over 20%. Vegetation is the second largest food source for animal 2, forming a third of the diet, with fish representing 17%.

Best approach to description – Say what the charts show. Describe the main similarities, then the main differences.

C Key points – Animal 1 and animal 2 have a very similar spread of habitats. Tropical forest is the main habitat for both animals – around 50% of each species is to be found there. 25–30% of both animals are found in temperate forest, just under 20% in grasslands, and less than 5% in tundra. Animal 3 is most commonly found in grasslands (over 40%) and temperate forest (about 35%). Just over 10% of animal 3 are found in tundra, and just under 10% in tropical forest.

Best approach to description – Say what the bar charts show. Describe the similarities in data for animals 1 and 2 together. Then contrast with the data for animal 3.

Think, plan, write

6 Possible answers

Describe the dominance of Asia, Europe and South America. Contrast the fall in Europe with the rise in Asia and South America. Describe the small catches for the remaining countries. Contrast the falls for Central America / the Caribbean and North America with rises in the other regions. Conclude with the point that overall world captures have increased by approximately 700 thousand tonnes.

Help yourself page 128

The final page in each unit is intended to raise a variety of extra areas that students can explore and to encourage responsibility for their own language learning.

Easily confused words

1 Key

a affects, effect
b desert, dessert
c definitive, definite
d excepted, accepted
e continual, continuous

2 Possible nswers

You need to stay in the shade during the hottest part of the day.

Your shadow gets longer as the sun gets lower in the sky.

I'm putting my car keys in your handbag – I don't want to lose them.

These trousers are so loose. They're going to fall down!

The economic forecast for the next six months isn't very good.

It's much more economical to buy a return train ticket than two singles.

I like to lie down for half an hour after a big meal.

Can you lay that blanket on the bed in the back room, please?

3 Key

a councillors. *Counsellors* are people who are trained to give advice to people with problems

b allowed. *Aloud* means in a voice that other people can hear.

c formally. *Formerly* means in earlier times or previously.

d tail. A *tale* is a story, especially an imaginative or exciting one.

e site. *Sight* means the ability to see, the act of seeing, or something that can be seen.

4 Key

past refers to something that has already happened; *passed* is the past simple form of the verb pass, and refers to the movement of passing.

a *principle* is a rule or strong belief that influences your actions; a *principal* is the head of a school or university

who's is a shortened form meaning *who is*; *whose* is a relative pronoun used to indicate possession

break means to damage something; *brake* means to slow down a machine, e.g. a car or bicycle

they're is a shortened form of *they are*; *their* means *of* or *belonging to them*.

a *roll* is something wrapped around itself, e.g. a roll of carpet; a *role* is an actor's part or a position in an organization

its is a possessive determiner meaning of or belonging to a thing; *it's* is a shortened from of *it is*.

5 Key

a The only **means** of transport is an infrequent bus service.

b On average, industrial workers **earn** less than $20,000 per year.

c Last year there was little trade **between** the two countries.

d A large **number** of scientists took part in the study.

e **Foreigners** who wish to work in that country require visas.

IELTS to do list

Encourage the students to tick one of the boxes and plan to do this task outside class.

Where to look

Students can use these practical tips to find further information.

11 Psychology

Introduction page 129

Issues – This section introduces the overall theme of the unit, focusing on personal psychology.

Aims – Students are given opportunities to think and speak about personality types.

1 Ask students to work in pairs or groups to discuss questions a–c.

Possible answers

a Some people are very relaxed in the company of others, while others can appear quite tense. In photo 1, the man is smiling and appears sociable, but the woman seems more reserved. In photo 2, the people look very relaxed in each other's company as they are sitting close to one another and are laughing or smiling. They are mainly looking at the girl on the left, who may have made a joke. In photo 3, the boy is looking away from the girl in the background, as though he feels isolated or wants to be by himself.

c A person's sociability is strongly affected by their personality type, for example whether they are introvert or extrovert, shy or confident. Background is likely to be a key factor: for example, have they been encouraged to mix and socialize when they were young? Cultural norms also affect this type of behaviour. People in some cultures tend to be more social than others.

2 Ask students to work in pairs or groups to discuss questions a–c.

Possible answers

a Photo 1: Although the woman is smiling, she looks slightly detached, as she is not making eye contact with the man. The man, in contrast, is looking directly at her, but there appears to be a lot of tension around his eyes and mouth. This suggests that he may not be relaxed and may not be showing his true feelings.
Photo 2: This group of people seem very much at ease and confident with each other. The man in the middle has an open posture. However, the others are sitting in more closed positions but leaning forward as though they want to be closer. The woman on the left is looking straight ahead while the others are mainly looking at her, suggesting that she may have made a comment

they are responding to or be the subject of someone else's comments.
Photo 3: The young man has turned his back on the woman in the background, suggesting that he does not wish to communicate with her. His facial expression, with slightly narrowed eyes, seems to indicate sadness or possibly anger. Although you can't see the girl very well she seems to be looking at him.

b Photo 1: woman – timid, anti-social; man – nervous
Photo 2: woman on left – confident; man in the middle – easy going; the other women and men – sociable
Photo 3: man – anti-social

Extra activity

Write the following sentence on the board. *David thought he was the best at everything and loved to tell people about all his great achievements.* Ask students to decide which word from exercise 3b it matches. Tell students to choose four more words from these exercises and write a sentence to go with each. They then swap sentences with a partner and try to match each sentence with the correct word.

Reading page 130

Issues – This section introduces the topic of sensory illusions.

Aims – Students practise finding specific information and study text organization

Orientation

1 Key

a sight, smell, taste, touch, hearing
b acidic: taste
perfume: smell
perfume: smell
beauty: sight
rough: touch
deafening: hearing
salty: taste
gas: smell
sticky: touch
whisper: hearing
yellow: sight

Possible answers

Other words associated with the senses:
sight: clashing, glowing, sombre, colourful, vision, image, observation, visibility
smell: fragrant, stale, acrid, odourless, aroma, scent, stink, nostril
taste: sweet, spicy, sour, creamy, sip, nibble, lick, appetite
touch: tingling, smooth, bumpy, sharp, contact, stroke, fingertip, pressure
hearing: shrill, booming, rhythmic, deep, high-pitched, eardrum, silence, hush

Finding specific information

2 Key

The results can help people who have had limbs amputated overcome physical discomfort in their phantom limbs. (Paragraph 5)

Text organization

4 Key

Paragraphs 1–4: The experiments and the explanation
Paragraph 5: Practical application
Paragraphs 6–7: Philosophical implications

IELTS practice
Questions 1–4: Classifying statements

Key

1 B. They discovered *the object your helper touches does not even need to resemble your hand* (lines 28–29).
2 A. They believe *this illusion is strong enough to overcome the discrepancy between the position of your real hand that you can feel and the site of the plastic hand you can see* (lines 22–25).
3 C. They learned that *if you 'threaten' the table by aiming a blow at it, the person winces and even starts sweating* (lines 41–42).
4 A. They suggested *the similarity in appearance fools the brain into mistaking the false hand for your real hand* (lines 20–22).

Questions 5–7: Multiple-choice questions

Key

5 A. The text says *It is as if the table becomes incorporated into a person's own body image so that it is linked to emotional centres in the brain*(lines 45–47). B is false because although how people react may be a reflex action triggered by the movement of the other person's hand, this in itself does not explain why subjects respond in the way they do to the table being threatened. Electrical skin resistance is mentioned, but not an electrical connection, so C is false. D, the idea that the table is one of the subject's possessions, is not mentioned.

6 B. The author states that *the brain makes these judgements about the senses automatically: they do not involve conscious thought* (lines 73–75). A is false because of the last part of that statement *these processes do not involve conscious thought*. C is false because the text says *this mechanism seems to be based on automatic processes that our intellect cannot override* (lines 71–73). D is false because the text says *perception is based largely* (not only) *on matching up sensory inputs* (line 65).

7 B. The text states that *One premise that seems to be beyond question is that you are anchored in your body. Yet given a few seconds of the right kind of stimulation, even this obvious fact is temporarily forsaken* (lines 82–86). A may be true, but the experiments were inspired by the work with patients, rather than the other way round. C is false because the text does not say this, just that some of our beliefs *can be called into question*. D is false because the text states that *the brain makes ... judgements about the senses automatically; they do not involve conscious thought* (lines 73–75).

Questions 8–13: Summary completion

Key

8 limbs (line 51)
9 cramp (line 62)
10 mirror (line 56)
11 intact (line 57)
12 reflection (line 60)
13 relieving (line 62)

Exploration

5 Key

a dummy corporation = a fake company usually set up for a dishonest purpose such as money laundering
b dummy run = a trial before the real thing
c dummy pills = placebos, or tablets used as a substitute for medicine
d dummy security cameras = security cameras which look real but do not take pictures, and which are intended to have a deterrent effect on criminals.

6 Key

a tap = to touch or hit quickly and gently e.g. Tap someone on the shoulder.
  stroke = to move your hand gently over something. e.g. Stroke someone's hair.
  other verbs: touch, stroke, pat, tap, knock, hit, punch, strike
b strange = uncanny
c phantom limbs = limbs that someone imagines they have but in fact do not have. Common meaning: ghost

d People *wince* when they feel pain or remember something painful or embarrassing; people *sweat* when they are very hot or nervous.

7 Possible answers

In hot weather people see mirages. These are apparent patches of water on a road which is in reality dry.

When sitting in a stationary train, if you look out of the window at a moving train nearby, the stationary train can appear to be moving.

If you touch cold water with a very cold hand, it can appear to be hot.

Taste and smell, because they are closely linked, can become confused to create illusions. For example an everyday food item can taste different from usual because it is affected by a strong smell or a head cold, for example.

8 Key

Fading dot

You may not be aware of it, but your eye constantly makes rapid movements. Each time it moves, your eye receives new information and sends it to your brain. You need this constant new information to see images. Although the dot fades, everything else in your field of vision remains clear. That's because everything else you see has distinct edges.

Bird in cage

The birds you see here are 'afterimages', images that remain after you have stopped looking at something. Your eye is lined with cells, called cones, which are sensitive to certain colors of light. When you stare at the red bird, your red-sensitive cones lose their sensitivity, so that when you look at the white bird cage, you see white, minus red, where the red-sensitive cones have adapted. White light minus red light is blue-green light. This is why the afterimage you see is blue-green. When you stare at the green bird, the green-sensitive cones adapt. White light minus green light is magenta light, so you see a magenta afterimage.

Listening page 134

Issues – This section introduces the topic of psychometric testing.

Aims – Students are given opportunities to discuss personality testing, before practising a series of exam tasks on the topic.

Orientation

1 Check that students know the meaning of *meticulous* (paying careful attention to detail), *articulate* (good at expressing ideas in words), *animated* (full of interest and energy), *harmonious* (friendly, without disagreement), *amicable* (polite and friendly), *empathetic* (with sensitivity for another's feelings) and *gregarious* (liking to be with other people).

2 Possible answers

c People take tests like these because they might be required to for a job. Alternatively they may want to have their own ideas confirmed by 'experts' because they believe these tests provide reliable, objective information. Another use is to find out what type of job would suit them.

d Information from tests like these can be used to supplement information from interviews, educational qualifications and other sources. The tests can convey information on personality and aptitude for a job or course which may be difficult to obtain by other means.

IELTS practice
Questions 1–5: Sentence completion

Key

1 selection procedure	4 ratings
2 assessments	5 objective
3 administer	

Questions 6–7: Multiple-choice questions

Key

6 B. The lecturer says *The overall purpose of the tests is to identify personality leanings or inclinations ... rather than fixed qualities, ... or ... character weaknesses.* So B is the correct answer and A and C are false.

7 B. The lecturer tells us that *The effectiveness of any method which asks questions, of course, is heavily dependent on the individual's willingness to answer a set of standard questions.* Standard questions are mentioned, but not the standard of questions, so A is false. C is not mentioned.

Questions 8–10: Short answer questions

Key

8 four
9 decision making
10 structured, flexible

Recording script

Lecturer: Hello. My name is Alexandra Blaby and today I'll be talking about one of the ways in which personality can be assessed: 'psychometric testing'. Psychometric literally means 'measuring the mind', and there are many carefully constructed tests which attempt to carry out this process. Probably the most common use for these tests is to help people find out the careers that most suit their personality. **Many employers ask new job applicants to take a psychometric or personality test as part of their selection procedure.** One of the features of this type of test is that there are no right or wrong answers to the questions. For this reason, **it would be more accurate to call them assessments rather than tests**. There are four main types of personality test currently in use. These are questionnaires, ratings tests, projective tests, and objective tests. Let's start by considering questionnaires, as these are by far the most common method. Here subjects are asked between fifty and a hundred questions about themselves. A typical question might be 'Do you enjoy spending time alone?' There are two advantages to questionnaires: firstly, **they are easy to administer**, and secondly, the questions are answered by the person who knows the subject best – themselves. By contrast, **a ratings test is done by someone who knows the subject well**, rather than the subjects themselves. A rater might be asked, for example, to agree or disagree with a statement about the subject. A typical statement might be: 'He laughs a lot.' The effectiveness of ratings tests depends on how well the rater knows the subject. Projective tests ask the subject to make sense of information which is unclear in some way. In the famous 'inkblot test', for example, subjects have to say what a patch of ink on a piece of paper looks like to them. Finally, **objective tests. In these tests the subject has to engage in a physical activity**. How they do it will tell the tester something about their personality. For example, the subject might be asked to blow up a balloon until it bursts. From observing how the subject does this, the tester will be able to say how timid or brave he or she is. Perhaps at this stage, we should clarify what exactly we learn about people from psychometric tests. **The overall purpose of the tests is to identify personality leanings or inclinations rather than fixed qualities or, as some people fear, character weaknesses.** This explains why tests often include several similar questions. How consistently the subject answers these will enable the tester to reach an accurate assessment. Incidentally, the assessment procedure may be carried out by a psychologist or another trained individual, but is most frequently done automatically by a computer. **The effectiveness of any method which asks questions, of course, is heavily dependent on the individual's willingness to answer a set of standard questions.** One of the most well-respected psychometric tests is the Myers–Briggs test, which asks subjects about their preferences in **four main areas**. Firstly the test asks people where they direct their energy: to the outer world of activity or the inner world of thoughts and emotions. Secondly, people are asked how they prefer to process information: in the form of known facts or in the form of possibilities. **The third area is decision making**: do people make decisions on the basis of logic or of personal values. Lastly Myers–Briggs tests ask people how they prefer to organize their lives – **in a structured or a flexible way**. Although there are those who disapprove of personality testing, there is no doubt that it is here to stay. Human beings have always been curious to find out about themselves and others: psychometric testing gives them an objective, scientific means of doing this. Well, that's all for today. Tomorrow I'll be examining ways of measuring intelligence ...

Speaking page 136

Aims – Students learn to describe the benefits of their hobbies, which will be useful for Part 1 Speaking.

Orientation

1 Possible answers

a People who collect unusual things might be organized, obsessive, or systematic.
   Those who play music are probably artistic and creative. People who restore old objects might be practical and have perfectionist tendencies.

b Free-time activities may offer a complete change or break from the pressures of work. For example involvement in sport allows people to use excess energy and work off aggression. If their work involves close and stressful contact with others, people might choose a solitary free-time activity to get some peace and quiet.

Describing interests

2 Key

a Speaker 1: collecting things
   Speaker 2: playing an instrument
   Speaker 3: restoring old objects

b Speaker 1: has made friends and visited places. He says it's a real change from his job
   Speaker 2: makes a little money, has good fun, and spends time with friends. It is also relaxing.
   Speaker 3: finds her hobby lucrative (money-making).

Recording script

Speaker 1 **I do various things in my free time**, but **my passion is collecting** Coke cans. I've got nearly 800 different ones, from all over the world. I belong to a soft drinks container collecting group which has members in 47 different countries. Apart from the language printed on cans from different countries, it's amazing how different the designs are. There are the normal everyday cans, but there are also special commemorative cans they produce for big events like the Olympic games. **I've made loads of new friends through my hobby** and even visited a couple of them – and it's a real change from the work I do as a supermarket manager.

Speaker 2: **I spend nearly all my free time** playing with a jazz quartet – I play the drums. We started off as a school band, and just kept going. We play for private parties and in bars – about twice a week. **We even get paid** for

some of the bookings we do – not that any of us do it for the money. **For me, it's just good fun – a chance to be with my mates and relax** doing something different.

Speaker 3: **I'm into restoring antique furniture in a big way**. It all started when I mended an old chair for my grandparents. It took me ages to do, but it was quite interesting. To do it properly you have to find out about different kinds of wood, as well as learning a whole range of techniques like carving, planing and polishing. There's more to it than people think. Since that first chair, I've repaired tables, cupboards, all sorts of things – even clocks for friends, and friends of friends. **It's actually quite a lucrative hobby** probably because there aren't that many people around who can do it properly – I'm even thinking of turning it into my full-time job.

3 Key

What I do
I do various things in my spare time (Speaker 1)
I spend nearly all my free time (Speaker 2)
I'm into … in a big way. (Speaker 3)
My passion is... (Speaker 1)
How I benefit
For me, it's just good fun. (Speaker 2)
I've made loads of new friends through my hobby. (Speaker 1)
It's a chance to be with my mates. (Speaker 2)
It's a real change from … (Speaker 1)
It's quite a lucrative hobby. (Speaker 3)

Language for writing page 137

Aims – Students revise the use of articles which is a crucial aspect of accurate writing.

Articles

1 Key

All the words in italics are nouns.

2 Key

a Despite fears, people with mental health problems rarely use **violence**.

b Not everyone has **the courage** to admit when they have made a mistake.

c We are currently carrying out **an investigation** into anti-depressants. **The investigation** is likely to last at least a year.

d The team were doing **research** into how well crows can solve problems.

e Online journals are read mostly by **academics**.

3 Key

  a Because *violence* is referring to a general abstract idea and therefore behaves like a singular noun.

  b Because *the courage* refers to a particular type or degree of courage, in this case the courage to do something.

  c *An* is used for the first time *investigation* is mentioned, *the* when it is mentioned again.

  d *Research* is uncountable.

  e You could add a relative clause, e.g. ... the academics who are engaged in active research.

Abstract nouns

4 Key

a Honesty	e the intelligence
b Behaviour	f Information
c the honesty	g intelligence
d the behaviour	h the information

Uncountable nouns

5 Key

Adding an expression of quantity makes them countable.
a piece of advice, work, rubbish
a bit of help, knowledge luck,
an item of news
a sum of money

Articles and adjectives

6 Key

  a the wild

  b The rich / The wealthy / The well off

  c The unemployed

  d the unknown

  e The blind

Writing page 138

Aims – Students revise common errors which may cause them difficulties in their writing.

Common errors

1 Key

Extract a: singular / plural agreement
More choice **is** not always better than less. The more alternatives there **are** when we make a selection the less satisfaction we derive from our ultimate decision.
Extract b: word order
Many members of the animal kingdom will **readily help** immediate family, but humans alone extend altruism beyond this, **regularly helping** strangers for no personal gain.
Extract c: spelling
Psychiatrists label someone as delusional when they have a false view of reality, **believing** falsehoods with total conviction. Evidence against the delusion will not shake **their** view.
Extract d: articles
People **with synaesthesia** have their senses mixed or overlapping. For example, a visual stimulus will also cause them to **hear sound**. It is not normally thought to be an indication **of poor** health, and some synaesthetes say they enjoy the experience.

Punctuation

2 Key

  a an apostrophe

  b a comma

  c a comma

  d a full stop

  e a colon

  f an apostrophe

3 Key

It's a classic philosopher's conundrum: how does my perception of the world, which only I can experience, differ from yours? Take a red rose, for example. We can probably agree it's red rather than blue, but what exactly is red? Do I see the same red as you? Philosophers have been wrestling with this question for centuries, and sensory scientists too have long been interested in why people report such different experiences of the same colours, odours or flavours. The question is whether it is purely subjective or based on some objective difference in their sensory experiences.

Help yourself page 140

The final page in each unit is intended to raise a variety of extra areas that students can explore and to encourage responsibility for their own language learning.

Planning remedial work

1 Explain to students that the purpose of this section is to plan how they can most effectively improve their language skills and not to criticize them for any difficulties they may have. The more honest students can be about their difficulties the greater chance they will have of improving.

4 All of these suggestions could prove useful to students, but different things will work better for different learners.

IELTS to do list

Encourage the students to tick one of the boxes and plan to do this task outside class.

Where to look

Students can use these practical tips to find further information.

12 Engineering and innovation

Introduction page 141

Issues – This section introduces the overall theme of the unit, focusing on the effects of innovations and inventions on people's lives.

Aims – Students are given opportunities to think and speak about a range of topics linked to engineering and innovation, learning relevant vocabulary along the way.

1 Ask students to work in pairs or groups to discuss the pictures. Check that students know the meaning of *innovative* (using new ideas or ways of doing things).

Possible answers

Photo 1: The Petronas Towers, Kuala Lumpur, Malaysia. It is made prinicipally from steel-reinforced concrete. The main challenge in building it was the need for very deep foundations (120m) requiring massive amounts of concrete.

Photo 2: One of the Palm Islands, off the coast of Dubai. It is made from rocks and sand (50 million cubic metres). The main challenges in building it were reclaiming land from a depth of 10 metres and building a connecting road to the mainland in order to transport materials.

Photo 3: The Millau Bridge, France. It is constructed of concrete and steel. The main challenges in building it included extremes of temperature and high cross-winds.

2 Ask students to work in pairs or groups to discuss the questions.

Possible answers

concrete: this material has made it possible to build much larger and stronger structures; negatives – it has arguably led to a lot of uninspiring architecture.

bicycle: this has provided a completely environmentally-friendly and low-cost form of transport.

telephone: it provided the first form of instant worldwide communication; negatives – some people use the telephone as a substitute for real, face-to-face communication.

gunpowder: a useful material in the construction and mining industries; negatives – has led to enormous loss of life due to use in weaponry.

fibre optics: the development of fibre optics has revolutionized modern telecommunications.

steel: an important material for the construction industry and many other industries such as automobile and ship-building; negatives – a limited natural resource which consumes large quantities of energy in its production.

aerosol: highly convenient as a means of storing a huge range of semi-liquids; negatives – it is harmful to the environment, as aerosol gases damage the ozone layer.

jet engine: it has revolutionized modern transport, enabling people to travel huge distances in a relatively short time; negatives – jet fuel is a major environmental pollutant.

nuclear power: a relatively cheap and non-polluting form of energy which consumes only moderate quantities of natural resources; negatives – nuclear radiation can cause devastating environmental damage and loss of life, nuclear weapons have killed hundreds of thousands of people and threaten the lives of millions more.

clock / watch: the widespread introduction of clocks and watches dramatically changed the way societies were run, allowing far greater efficiency in the regulation of working hours, transportation, schools, etc.; negatives – people became slaves to time, losing a lot of personal freedom.

light bulb: homes and workplaces became much brighter, more cheerful, easier to live and work in; negatives – it became far easier for people to work unsocial hours, the peace of the countryside is increasingly disturbed by bright lights.

petrol / diesel engine: an important fuel for private and public transport, which has provided a huge increase in personal mobility; negatives – a major source of atmospheric pollution.

air conditioning: has provided comfortable living and working environments in hot and humid locations around the world; negatives – it uses a large amount of energy, and has been implicated as a carrier of unhealthy bacteria.

sound amplifier: a major component of modern music and all types of recording, it also enables people to address huge live audiences; negatives – a major source of noise pollution.

television: probably the most significant development in entertainment of the past 100 years, a great source of comfort and information to billions of people around the world; negatives – a very passive form of entertainment which has arguably made the average person lazier and more socially isolated, and has allowed dominant cultures to have an undue influence over minority ones.

3 Ask students to work in pairs or groups to discuss these questions.

Possible answers

c Innovations such as texting catch on because they are convenient and have broad appeal. Texting has proved a very convenient means of communication, so much so that it has been recognized by people of all ages. It is also a relatively cheap way of communicating. Other products, such as wrist TVs are expensive, are not really practical and not many people can see the benefit of having one. It is probably an item which is brought many for its status value.

Reading page 142

Issues – This section introduces the topic of tensegrity, a sculptural form that combines art, engineering and biology.

Aims – Students study text organization and apply it to IELTS classification questions.

Orientation

1 Key

a art and engineering   b triangles

Text organization

3 Make sure students read the Note before they complete the exercise.

Key

works of art: paragraphs A–B
biology research: paragraphs E–G
engineering and architecture: paragraphs C–D

4 Key

1 E–G   2 A–B   3 C–D

IELTS practice
Questions 1–3: Classification

Key

1 C. The text states that *five years later ... [than 1988] ... scientists described the tensegrity model of cell structure* (line 50–52).
2 B. The text says that Snelson had started with *an abstract sculpture* (line 10) and in 1949, *had perfected a concept in which stiff rods can be supported without touching by a network of wires* (lines 13–14).
3 C. The text says that *in the 1980s, tensegrity architecture began to appear ... the first important structure was his Gymnastics Hall at the Korean Olympics in 1988* (line 46–49).

Questions 4–10: Locating information

Key

4 D. *It took some time to prove him wrong* (lines 45–46).
5 E. *... its significance in quite a different field became apparent when scientists described the tensegrity model of cell structure, and this is where the principle is now making waves. ... biologists ...* (lines 50–58)
6 D. *It is strange that architects and engineers didn't discover the principle before 1948* (line 37).
7 B. *Using an abstract sculpture as a starting point, Snelson then added tension wires to the free floating members* (lines 10–11).
8 G. *Whether or not the cell is a tensegrity structure is still controversial* (line 75–76).
9 C. *Although drinking straws are weak ... it resists the pressure* (lines 26–34).
10 F. *The human body is certainly a tensegrity structure: it consists of 206 bones – tensegrity rods ...* (lines 60–61)

Questions 11–14: Short-answer questions

Key

11 (Buckminster) Fuller (line 15)
12 tension bands / rubber bands (line 23)
13 microfilaments (line 64)
14 (proteins called) integrins (line 72)

Exploration

5 Key

a being squeezed: compression (line 4)
b being stretched: tension (line 4)
c not bending: stiff (line 13)
d weaken and bend under pressure: buckle (line 26)
e having two halves which are exactly the same: symmetrical (line 32)
f falling inwards: collapsing (line 54)
g having moving parts: mechanical (line 56)
h tightly stretched: taut (line 73)

6 Key

a 5   b 3   c 7   d 1   e 4   f 2   g 6

7 Key

a pick ... off   e wired up
b falling apart   f bounced back
c take part   g fling ... around
d go on

8 Possible answers

c A light and airy building could give a feeling of lightness and optimism. Similarly, a building with large, open rooms could create a sense of space and freedom. However, an over-complex design could create a feeling of frustration and a cramped building could give a feeling of claustrophobia. If the a building were dark, it could cause feelings of depression.

d A beehive: the honeycomb pattern could be used for interlocking rooms. Insect wings: a building could be designed with sliding roof panels that fold back like the wings of a fly. A tree: the shape of a tree and branches could be imitated to construct an 'organic' wooden house.

Listening page 146

Aims – Students learn to predict the kind of information required for short-answer questions.

Orientation

1 Key

a Photo 1: A hand-held global positioning satellite (GPS) unit, used to give precise location information. Satellites in orbit send out time signals and by monitoring the signals, and by applying complex calculations, it is possible to work out exact position anywhere on the planet.
Photo 2: Snow and ice climbing tools, used for mountain climbing on snow- and ice-covered mountains. These tools can break through hard packed snow and ice to provide grip and carve out handholds and footholds for climbers.
Photo 3: Portable water filter, used to clean impurities from water to make it drinkable. A ceramic filter with a very tiny pore size stops the passage of harmful bacteria. The filter is impregnated with silver to kill off micro-organisms.
Photo 4: Omniglow light sticks, used for camping and hiking, navigation on sea and land, and also as decoration. Light is generated by the chemical reaction of two fluids mixing.

b GPS unit: useful on any walking, mountaineering or exploring expedition.

Climbing tools: useful on any mountaineering expedition above the snow-line.
Water filter: useful on any hiking or mountaineering expedition, or when travelling in a country where clean drinking water is generally unavailable.
Light sticks: useful on any camping or hiking expedition.

c GPS unit: people used a map and magnetic compass, or possibly the stars.
Climbing tools: people used wooden implements.
Water filter: people used water purifying tablets.
Light sticks: people used torches, gas lamps, or candles.

Possible answers

d Food, dried or tinned, for nourishment.
A multi-purpose penknife, to prepare food.
Matches or some other way to light a fire or stove.
A portable stove, to prepare food.
A sleeping bag for warmth.
A tent for shelter.
A map, to use with the GPS unit.
A whistle, to attract attention if you get lost.

Thinking ahead

2 Key

It's a waterproof watch which can be used as a transmitting device to send an emergency signal. It has two separate mechanisms to keep it powered up: one is quartz electronic with an LCD digital display, and the other is a self-winding mechanical system that turns the hands.

3 Key

1 price   4 distance
2 place name   5 weight
3 length of time 6 date (probably year or century)

IELTS practice
Questions 1–6: Short-answer questions

Key

1 £20,000   4 160 kilometres
2 Antarctica   5 85 grams
3 48 hours   6 1770

Questions 7–10: Labelling a diagram

Key

7 crystal   9   transmitter battery
8 crown   10 antenna

Recording script

Sandy: Good afternoon. I'm Sandy Raymond and I'm going to be talking about a remarkable timepiece called the Breitling Emergency Watch. Some of you may remember it as the watch that Richard Branson auctioned off on eBay, raising **£20,000** for charity, after he'd lent it to Steve Fossett for his non-stop round the world flight. Perhaps more significantly, though, it was the kind of watch being worn last year by two British pilots whose helicopter crashed into the sea just off **Antarctica**. Finding themselves in a lifeboat with no other means of communication, they activated the transmitters inside their watches. The signals were picked up by a Chilean aircraft, which homed in on them and then organized a rescue that saved the men's lives. And these are just the people the watch was designed for: aviators and air crew who suddenly find themselves on the ground or in the water after a forced landing. The watch has a built-in microtransmitter which can broadcast a signal for up to **48 hours** on 121 point 5 megahertz, the aircraft emergency frequency. It's water resistant, too. Even with the transmitter operating, it can be used at depths of up to 30 metres. The operating range depends to a great extent on whether there are any obstacles between the transmitter and the rescue aircraft. On flat terrain with few trees, for instance, the signal can be picked up at up to **160 kilometres** away, and **it's the same on water** as long as the seas are calm, while from the top of a mountain it has a range of up 400 kilometres. It's not a particularly bulky or heavy item to wear, though: at 16 millimetres thick and measuring 43 in diameter, it's just **85 grams**, which is about the normal weight for this kind of wrist watch. So, what makes this watch tick, as it were? The answer to that is two separate mechanisms: one quartz electronic with an LCD digital display, and the other a self-winding mechanical system that turns the hands. This is driven by an oscillating weight that swings in time with the movements of the wrist, thus creating the energy to rewind the watch automatically. I should point out here that this is hardly a new invention, as it dates back to **1770** when the Frenchman Abraham-Louis Perrelet first made a watch of this kind. Incidentally, an example of his work is still keeping good time today, over two hundred years later.

Let's take a look inside an Emergency Watch. Possibly the first thing you notice at the top is the gold ring indicating compass points and degrees. This surrounds the **crystal**, which looks like glass but is in fact made of a scratch-proof synthetic material. On a scale of one to ten, with ten as diamond hardness, this scores nine. So the crystal fits onto a protective case made of titanium, a hard but light antimagnetic metal that is also used in the manufacture of high-performance aircraft. On the right-hand side of the inner case is the **crown**, used for setting the time and the date. This rounded knob has a locking device to prevent moisture or dust getting into the watch. The watch itself, with the two independent timing systems I mentioned before, is kept separate from the other components. This means that even if the timekeeping functions are damaged in a crash, the emergency signal can still keep going out. For this reason there are two batteries, an upper one for the watch and a **transmitter battery** below which fits neatly into the circuit board. All the above are housed in the outer case, which in the case of the version shown is made of gold alloy. On the right of this case you'll notice a rounded cap, which looks like a winding knob, but isn't. This is the real 007 bit: if you twist the cap anticlockwise and then pull to its full extent, the cap comes off and you have a 43-centimetre **antenna**, which immediately starts transmitting on 121.5 megahertz. Incidentally, on the other side of the case there's a secondary antenna which can also be extended, thereby increasing the range of the transmitter.

Speaking page 148

page 148

Aims – Students learn useful language for describing objects, which may be needed for Speaking Part 2.

Describing objects

1 Key

Item 3

2 Key

SHAPE: vertical, upright
HOW IT WORKS: electronic
TEXTURE: smooth
IMPRESSION IT GIVES: elegant
MATERIAL: plastic
COLOUR: black, sky-blue

3 Key

SHAPE: rounded, flat
TEXTURE: soft, rough
MATERIAL: metal, wooden
COLOUR: bluey-green, reddish
HOW IT WORKS: manual, mechanical
IMPRESSION IT GIVES: intriguing, cute

4 Possible answers

Item 1 is for brushing your teeth. It's designed to experiment with new variations on a standard toothbrush. It's made of wood and bristle. It looks a bit like a set of false teeth.

Item 2 is for drinking. It's designed to be held with both hands to avoid spillages. It's made of orange plastic. It looks a bit like a pair of glasses with a false nose attached.

Item 4 is for watering plants. It's designed to amuse and show technological innovation. It's made of plastic. It looks a bit like a vase.

IELTS practice

Part 2: Extended speaking

5 Make sure students read the Note before they complete the task. Tell students they are going to practise a Speaking Part 2 task. Remind them to write about each point listed, using notes and not full sentences.

6 Students work in pairs. Ask them to time each other if possible and make a note of how long their partner spoke for.

Language for writing page 149

page 149

Aims – Students revise expressions for expressing purpose, and cause and effect, both of which are important for a range of academic writing.

Expressing purpose

1 Key

a so that   e in order to
b to   f for
c in order that   g in order not to
d for

2 Key

a so that, in order that   b to, in order to   c for

3 Key

a This radio uses an external aerial to pick up / in order to pick up / for picking up local stations.

b We are building smaller apartments in order that / so that they will be more popular.

c Solar panels don't always need bright sunshine to generate / in order to generate / for generating electricity.

d They use synthetic materials for less weight.

e Close down the computer properly in order not to / so that you don't / in order that you don't damage it.

Cause and effect

4 Key

Text A: a battery
Text B: a tap (US English: faucet)
Text C: a thermometer

5 Key

Text A: owing to, leads to, since, triggered
Text B: enables, because of, results in, in turn, consequently, lets
Text C: make, causes, created, therefore, forced, thus allowing

6 Key

a makes the construction stronger.
b Consequently / Therefore, the mechanism does not overheat.
c of effective airbags has led to fatal car accidents decreasing.
d the dial is luminous, it can be read at night.
e the brakes makes the machine slow down.
f to a valve closing, the correct pressure is maintained.

7 Possible answers

a New developments in nanotechnology will lead to electronic items getting even smaller in the future.

b Concerns about air pollution are forcing airlines to develop cleaner planes.

c Mistakes are frequently made by pharmacists owing to the poor handwriting of doctors who fill out prescriptions.

d A new design of football introduced this season enables the ball to be kicked further than last year.

e Growing traffic chaos has triggered an urgent need for new solutions.

f Increasing debt among the student population has resulted in far more students taking on part time jobs.

Extra activity

Write the following sentences on the board:

1 *They couldn't complete the building on time … the long delays.*

2 *The unusual increase in pressure in the main tank … the alarm system.*

3 *A steel construction is used … the maximum strength is achieved.*

4 *It is necessary to drain the system … carry out any maintenance.*

5 *The valve opens, … the air to enter the upper chamber.*

6 *The structure is built to the highest standards. …, it is extremely durable.*

Write the following list of words and phrases:
triggered in order to consequently thus allowing because of in order that

Ask students to complete the sentences with the correct words and phrases.

Key

1 because of   4 in order to
2 triggered   5 thus allowing
3 in order that   6 Consequently

Writing page 150

Aims – Students study different ways of organizing a description, such as may be required for Writing Task 1.

Orientation

1 Key

a a windsurfer, a hang-glider, a helicopter

Possible answers

b Windsurfer: You stand on the board, holding a bar connected to the sail. You turn the bar to face the sail into the wind, and allow the wind to carry you across the water.
Hang-glider: You hang in a harness attached under the wings, launch yourself into the air from high ground and control the movement of the glider by moving the frame from side to side.
Helicopter: A combustion engine drives the rotor blades on top of the vehicle. The movement of the helicopter is controlled by adjusting the pitch of the rotor blades from inside the cockpit.

c Easiest: windsurfer
Most difficult: helicopter

Organizing a description

2 Possible answers

a Describe the ways in which the solar panel generates and stores power during the day, then how power is released at night.

b Describe how the bicycle is designed, then how a rider uses it.

c Describe the first television, followed by major developments such as colour and stereo sound, then a modern television.

3 Make sure students read the Note before they complete the exercise. Ensure that students do not look ahead to exercise 4 at this stage, as it contains a full description of the diagrams.

Possible answers

The diagrams show a hot air balloon and the basic principles that enable it to be flown. See exercise 4.

4 Key

a It describes the main features of the balloon and their purposes, then how its movement is controlled.

b to (produce), to (carry), so that, in order to, to (heat)

c enable, as, causes, since, allows

Possible answers

d How to control the downward movement of the balloon has been omitted.
To make it descend, the pilot closes the burner, so that the supply of hot air to the envelope is cut off. Consequently, the air inside cools down, leading to it becoming as heavy as the air outside. This results in the balloon losing height.

Think, plan, write

6 Key

a The objects are in chronological order, covering a century.

b The common design features are: wings for lift, power source(s) for thrust, tail, space for crew / passengers.

c Douglas DC-3: This plane has two engines, instead of the one in the Wright Flyer, to provide more power. The engines are located on the wings, not inboard, to provide more stability.
Boeing Airbus A30: This plane has four engines instead of two, to provide yet more power. There are two passenger decks instead of one, to provide more space for passengers.

d Practical effects: Planes fly at higher altitudes, and at faster speeds, and more people travel by plane than before.
Trends: planes get longer, wingspans wider, engines more numerous and powerful.

Help yourself page 152

The final page in each unit is intended to raise a variety of extra areas that students can explore and to encourage responsibility for their own language learning.

Subject-specific vocabulary

1 Key

Health: disability, fertility, placebo effect
History and archaeology: artefact, excavate
Education: literacy skills, research
Society: birth rate, inequality, meritocracy, social mobility, taxation
Business and the workplace: absenteeism, commercial gain, income, investment, pension, productivity, target, workforce
Psychology: extroversion, illusion, perception, sensory

2 Key

a force = an effect that causes things to move in a particular way; general use – physical strength, violent action
bodies = groups or collections of things; general use – the physical structures of humans or animals

b sacrifice = a killing offered to a god as part of a ceremony; general use – giving something up

c capital = the amount of money invested in or owned by a business; general use – the main city of a country
liquid = easily be changed into cash; general use – a substance that flows freely, neither a solid nor a gas

d raw = unprocessed, in its natural state; general use – not cooked

e wireless = a system of sending and receiving signals (without wires); general use – an old-fashioned word for *radio*

3 Possible answers

Because in academic contexts there will always be a significant proportion of subject-specific vocabulary. In order to speak formally or to write or understand a piece of academic writing it is necessary to understand a considerable amount of subject-specific vocabulary.
By revising the vocabulary that appears in the different units of the book it should be possible to build up a bank of subject-specific vocabulary related to these topics.

IELTS to do list

Encourage the students to tick one of the boxes and plan to do this task outside class.

Where to look

Students can use these practical tips to find further information.

13 History and archaeology

Introduction page 153

Issues – This section introduces the overall theme of the unit, focusing on historic events of the last hundred years and the preservation of archaeological artefacts.

Aims – Students are given opportunities to think and speak about broad issues in history and archaeology.

1 Ask students to work in pairs or groups to discuss photos 1–4.

Key

a Photo 1: the fall of the Berlin wall
   Photo 2: Lenin, probably addressing a crowd
   Photo 3: the Beatles, waving to fans, probably at an airport
   Photo 4: the first man on the moon – American astronaut, Neil Armstrong
b 2, 3, 4, 1

Extra activity

Write the following list of events and social changes on the board. Students work in pairs or groups. Ask them to group the events into five pairs, two each for the 1950s, 1960s, 1970s, 1980s and 1990s.

John F Kennedy assassinated
Elvis Presley died
Hong Kong returned to China
John Lennon shot
The mini skirt invented
The Euro launched
Ronald Reagan became US president
DNA discovered
The Vietnam war ended

Key

1950s: DNA discovered (1953), 1960s: John F Kennedy Assassination (1963), The mini skirt invented (1965); 1970s: The Vietnam war ended (1973); 1980s: John Lennon shot (1980), Ronald Reagan becomes US president (1980); 1990s: Hong Kong returned to China (1997), The Euro launched (1999)

Reading page 154

Issues – This section introduces the topic of ancient civilizations, and focuses on a particular civilization, the Moche of Peru, which came to a mysterious end.

Aims – Students study text organization in order to help them answer a series of IELTS reading tasks.

Orientation

1 Check that students know the meaning of *legacy* (a situation that exists now because of what happened in the past).

Key

a, b, c

Picture 1: The Ancient Egyptian civilization, 3200 BC–332 BC, ruled by 30 successive dynasties of pharoahs. The civilization ended when Alexander the Great conquered Egypt in 332 BC. The Ancient Egyptians left a legacy including the great pyramids, knowledge of mathematics and other scientific methods, engineering and irrigation.

Picture 2: The Roman Empire, main period of influence 27 BC–AD 476. At the height of this period, the Empire stretched all around the Mediterranean and covered most of western and southern Europe. There are differing theories as to why the Roman Empire collapsed, including a breakdown of 'civic virtue', decadence and weakness caused by over-expansion. They left a legacy including the Latin language and Roman alphabet, the Julian calendar, a vast road network and a huge number of prominent buildings.

Picture 3: The Mongolian Empire, 1206–1368. Founded by Genghis Khan, a ruthless military leader. It became the largest land empire in history, covering 35 million square kilometres. The Empire began to decline after the death of Genghis Khan's son, who ruled until 1241. A series of weaker leaders gradually allowed the empire to disintegrate into separate empires and to fall more under the influence of China. They left a legacy including a united China, a unified central Asia, and set an example of religious tolerance.

Picture 4: The Aztec civilization, 1375–1521. They constructed large palaces and temples in which they worshipped many gods. They were defeated by the Spanish conquistador Hernan Cortes, supported by rival Mesoamerican tribes, and then wiped out by European diseases. They left a legacy including great temples, and the foundations of the modern Mexico City.

Text organization

2 Key

Section 1: paragraphs 1–3, the legacy of the Moche.
Section 2: paragraphs 4–6 (except end of 6), the first theory on the disappearance of the Moche.
Section 3: end of paragraph 6 and paragraphs 7–8, the second theory on the disappearance of the Moche.

3 Key

a Section 1   b Section 2   c Section 3

IELTS practice

Questions 1–5: True / False / Not given

Key

1 True. The first paragraph says *Others* (pyramids) *house the elaborate tombs of Moche leaders* (lines 14–15).
2 True. The text says *system of mud brick aqueducts … Many are still in use today* (lines 18–21).
3 Not Given. The author says many artefacts were discovered, including *precious stones*, but there are no references to actual money, coins etc (lines 28–30).
4 False. We are told *the Moche left no written record* (line 33).
5 False. The text tells us that *all the soldiers were dressed alike … a story not of war but ritual combat* (lines 42–46).

Questions 6–10: Note completion

Key

6 rain (lines 63–65)
7 (huge) sand (dunes) (lines 91–94)
8 climate (lines 97–98)
9 AD 650 (line 109)
10 fortresses (line 113)

Questions 11–13: Multiple-answer question

Key

11–13 (in any order)
B. This is true because we are told in paragraph five about the thirty years of wet weather followed by thirty years of drought. (lines 79–82) We are told further down in paragraph five and paragraph seven that *climatic disasters* had fatally destroyed the Moche.
C. This is true because paragraph seven tells us that *the leadership … had lost its control over the population* (lines 125–129).
F. This is also true. We are told that *villages and clan groups turned on each other…* and that ritual battles were replaced by *civil war* (lines 129–134).
A is not true because the text says archaeologists were unable to find *non-Moche military artefacts*. (lines 116–117). D is not mentioned and although the text refers to sacrifices it says they were about *making an unpredictable world more predictable* (lines 66–67).

Exploration

4 Key

a This is asked in paragraph four and refers to human sacrifice. It is answered in the rest of that paragraph, which explains the sacrifices were made at a time of wet weather to celebrate and/or encourage more rain.
b This is asked near the beginning of paragraphs five. It is answered in this paragraph and the following two. The answer appears to be given in paragraph five, but this is refuted in paragraph six, before the apparently definitive answer appears in paragraph seven: *they destroyed their own civilization*.
c This question, found in paragraph six, asks who they had been at war with and is answered at the end of the same paragraph. They had been at war with themselves.

5 Key

a wall paintings = murals (line 12)
b not connected with religion = secular (line 13)
c connected with religion = sacred (line 13)
d surviving parts = remains (line 17)
e dug holes in the ground = excavated (line 21)
f dug out of the ground = unearthed (line 22)
g objects of archaeological interest = artefacts (line 28)
h pictures on works of art = images (line 43)
I series of religious actions = ritual (line 46)

Listing page 158

Aims – Students practise predicting the kind of
information required for note and table
completion questions.

Orientation

1 Key

c Photo 1: (King of Egypt) Tutankhamen's death
mask. (Circa 1352 BC)
Photo 2: Chinese Qin Dynasty terracotta statue
of a kneeling archer. (Circa 221–206 BC)
Photo 3: Ancient Egyptian pre-dynastic ivory hair
comb. (Circa 3500 BC)
Photo 4: Two Ancient Egyptian bronze daggers.
(Circa 16th–11th century BC)

Thinking ahead

3 Key

words: 1, 3, 4   numbers: 1, 2, 4

IELTS practice

Questions 1–4: Note completion

Make sure students read the Note before they
complete the task.

Key

1 free   3 flash or lights
2 twelve to five / 12–5   4 100 years

Recording script

Questions 1–4

Presenter: Welcome to the 'Museums UK' audio
series, a collection of downloadable
audio files introducing the best of
British museums. My name's Sam
Cooper and in this file I'll be
introducing the Ashmolean Museum of
Art and Archaeology in Oxford, with
its fabulous collections of Eastern and
Western Art, Antiquities, Casts and
Coins. It's one of the oldest public
museums in the world and it's actually
part of Oxford University, though **it's
free to go in**, whether you're a student
or not. You'll find the main museum in
Beaumont Street near the centre of
Oxford, close to both the railway
station and the bus station. Opening
hours for visitors are from ten o'clock
in the morning till five in the evening
on Tuesdays to Saturdays, **twelve to
five on Sundays**, and ten to seven on
Thursdays in the summer months. It
usually closes for three days over
Christmas, a couple of days at New

Year and three days for the St Giles
Fair in early September. You can take
photos in the galleries, but only with
hand-held cameras and **not using
flash or lights**, which can do serious
harm to exhibits. Also, as long you
follow all the copyright regulations and
you get permission from the staff on
duty, you can ask for antiquities
documents of **less than 100 years in
age** to be photocopied, at a cost of 5p
per A4 sheet.

Thinking ahead

4 Key

name of activity
length of activity
time and whether a.m. or p.m.
price
maximum number in a group

Questions 5–10: Table completion

Key

5 £4   8 one-fifteen / 1.15
6 14   9 workshops
7 50 minutes   10 £5

Recording script

Questions 5–10

Presenter: Perhaps not surprisingly given its links
with the University, the Ashmolean has
an Education Service for schools and
the general public. Activities include
guided group visits, which for adults
last sixty minutes and cost **four
pounds** each. This makes the
minimum price per group twenty-eight
pounds, as group sizes vary from seven
to fifteen people. Visits by groups of
young people take the same amount of
time as the adult tours, but cost just
two pounds for university students. So
with at least seven to a group the
lowest price is fourteen pounds,
though please note that there's an
upper limit of **fourteen** group
members rather than the fifteen for
adults. For schools, there are visits to
suit all age groups, and for the most
popular ones – such as those to see
the Greek and Egyptian collections –
it's best to book a term in advance.
Tours last **fifty minutes**, starting at
ten-fifteen, eleven-thirty and a quarter
past one, with a maximum of thirteen
children per group. Now if you're free
in the middle of the day, why not go
along to one of the 45-minute

lunchtime talks? There's a really wide range of topics. On the nineteenth, for example, the subject is 'Greek Mythology', and on the twentieth there's 'Celebration of India'. Both begin at **one-fifteen**, the usual time for these talks, and they're held every Tuesday, Wednesday and Friday. Another regular feature, on Saturday mornings through to the afternoons, are the **workshops**. If you're interested in developing your own illustrative and artistic skills, these are for you. They're aimed at artists of varying levels of experience, and are always led by practising artists. Running for six hours from ten o'clock, this is wonderful value at just **five pounds**, including basic materials – and also a decent cup of coffee.

Speaking page 160

Aims – Students study appropriate expressions for making contrasts between the past and the present, and put them into practice in a Speaking Part 3 task.

Changes over time

1 Possible answers

  a   Photo 1: A lamp-lighter lighting up a gas-powered street lamp. People had to manually turn on each lamp at dusk.
Photo 2: Women washing clothes in a lake. People had to wash clothes by hand.
Photo 3: A man playing a record on an old gramophone, while a child watches. People had to place the needle on the record and wind up the gramophone to make the record play.
  b   Photo 1: 1935, London, England. The fog, or smog, is a possible clue.
Photo 2: 1949, New York, USA. The distinctive New York skyline is a clue, as are the clothes worn by the women in the photo. (The photo shows 'Dry day' when people were encouraged to avoid using running water.)
Photo 3: 1947, England. The clothes are a possible clue.
  c   Photo 1: Automatic electronically operated street lighting.
Photo 2: Washing machines.
Photo 3: CD or MP3 players.

2 Key

Past	Present
Until quite recently ...	Nowadays ...
It was common to see ...	They no longer have to ...
Once, ...	Things are getting ...
In those days, ...	These days ...
They used to ...	Since then, ...
Back in..., they would ...	People are becoming ...

3 Possible answers

Back in the days before modern domestic appliances, people would wash clothes in rivers and lakes. They no longer have to go to such trouble – they just throw them into the washing machine. Once, people had to listen to music on old wind-up gramophones, but these days we have all kinds of different devices like CD players, walkmans and MP3 players.

IELTS practice
Part 3: Topic discussion

5 Remind students to use some of the contrasting expressions from exercise 2.

Language for writing page 161

Aims – Students revise features of conditionals, and learn important structures for use in academic writing.

Conditionals

1 Key

  a   will understand, read (future simple + present simple) = first conditional: used to describe a possible situation in the present or future
  b   had survived, would know (past perfect + conditonal + infinitive) = mixed conditional: used to describe an unreal past situation with imaginary present results
  c   loses, bends (present simple + present simple) = zero conditional: used to describe something that always happens
  d   had built, would have become (past perfect + conditional + have + past participle) = third conditional: used to describe an unreal past situation with imaginary past results
  e   used, would fade (past simple + conditional + infinitive) = second conditional: used to describe an unlikely or unreal situation in the present or future

2 Key

a provided that
b Supposing
c But for (= if not for)
d Providing
e on condition that
f unless (= if not)
g as long as
h Without (= if not / for)

3 Key

a museum were rich, it would be able to buy valuable objects.
b we dig deep enough, we may find a complete building.
c had not been a revolution, there would not be freedom in this country today.
d you have official permission, you will not be able to excavate here.
e had not improved, industrialization would not have taken place.
f as you know their address in 1851, you can learn more about your ancestors.
g the aid of modern technology, it would not have been possible to find the pharaoh's tomb.

4 Possible answers

a watercourses rather than roads would have become the main transportation routes.
b it might not have been discovered by Europeans for another two hundred years.
c we can avoid repeating the mistakes of the past.
d modern warfare would not exist.
e major human disasters will continue to occur.
f much of the world's population would have been wiped out by disease.
g the global economy should continue to grow.
h Europe would be 50 years behind Asia in economic development.

Writing page 162

Aims – Students practise the language of argument and hypothesis, and apply it to a Writing Task 2.

Orientation

1 Key

a fact: the first and second sentences
opinion: *these items should be returned to their countries of origin*

Argument and hypothesis

2 Key

1 e   2 d   3 c   4 b   5 f

3 Key

a conditional + infinitive
b second and third conditional
c Because they express the theoretical consequences of a course of action that has been taken or might be taken in future.

4 Possible answers

a If museum collections were lent to museums around the world, more people would be able to see the artefacts and learn about the civilizations they come from.
b If replica copies were made, these could replace the original in the museum, allowing the original to be returned to the country of origin. Alternatively, replicas could be provided to museums around the world that wished to display the artefacts, including a museum in the country of origin.

Help yourself page 164

The final page in each unit is intended to raise a variety of extra areas that students can explore and to encourage responsibility for their own language learning.

Pronunciation: individual sounds

1 Different students will have different problems with pronunciation, especially in multilingal classes. Encourage students to repeat all of them, but they should note the ones they have difficulty with and practise outside the class.

IELTS to do list

Encourage the students to tick one of the boxes and plan to do this task outside class.

Where to look

Students can use these practical tips to find further information.

14 Language

Introduction page 165

Issues – This section introduces the overall theme of the unit, focusing on the spread of English throughout the world.

Aims – Students are given opportunities to think and speak about broad issues related to language.

1 Ask students to work in pairs or groups to discuss questions a–d.

Possible answers

a It suggests that English is used as a universal langage and is used alongside local languages so signs can be understood by a wider audience.

c Most people would agree that their first language is an essential part of their personality and cultural identity.

2 Ask students to work in pairs or groups to discuss questions a–d.

Key

a café: French
paparazzi: Italian
ketchup: Chinese
fiasco: Italian

b Loan words are used because no exact word exists in the language, or because it is thought to be sophisticated or fashionable to use a foreign word.

Extra activity

Write the following lists of loan words on the board. Ask students to explain their meanings if possible, and to guess which language each list originates from.

A: *alligator, barricade, cannibal, ranch, tornado, vigilante*
B: *bungalow, juggernaut, loot, pyjamas, shampoo, thug*

Key

A: Spanish: alligator = a large reptile of the crocodile family
barricade = objects placed across a road to stop people from passing
cannibal = a person who eats human flesh
ranch = a large farm
tornado = a violent storm with circular winds
vigilante = an unauthorised person who tries to prevent crime

B: Hindi: bungalow = a single-storey house
juggernaut = a large lorry
loot = informal, money and valuables stolen by thieves
pyjamas = a loose jacket and trousers worn in bed
shampoo = liquid soap used for washing hair
thug = a violent person, especially a criminal

Reading page 166

Issues – This section introduces the topic of hyperpolyglottism, the ability to speak many languages.

Aims – Students practise scanning a text for specific information.

Orientation

1 Key

a The prefix *hyper-* means *very big, very great*, so *hyperpolyglot* means someone who can speak a large number of languages, not just two or three.

b He wants to know who holds the world record for the number of languages spoken and, presumably, how many languages they can speak.

c There seems to be no definitive answer, although some people think that the record is seventy-two, held by an Italian, Giuseppe Mezzofanti.

Scanning

2 Key

a   Dick Hudson, Loraine Obler, Philip Herdina, Stephen Krashen, Steven Pinker, Suzanne Flynn
b   CJ, Giuseppe Mezzofanti and Lomb Kato are all polyglots or hyperpoloyglots who have been subjects of study.
c   The academics who express opinions are: Loraine Obler, Philip Herdina, Stephen Krashen, Steven Pinker, Suzanne Flynn.

3 Key

Paragraphs 2, 3, 9 and 10

IELTS practice
Questions 1–5: Matching

Key

1   C Stephen Krashen. He maintains *that exceptional language learners simply work harder, and have a better understanding of how they learn* (lines 106–109).
2   B Philip Herdina. He doubts that *anyone has the capacity to speak seventy-two languages, arguing that maintaining this ability would take resources from other activities* (lines 78–81).
3   E Suzanne Flynn. According to her *There is no limit to the human capacity for language except for things like having time to get enough exposure to the language* (lines 84–88).
4   A Loraine Obler. The text suggests that to her ... *language talent was inborn and not related to a higher level of general intellectual ability* (lines 140–142).
5   D Steven Pinker. He maintains that *similar kinds of knowledge can interfere with one another* (lines 98–99).

Questions 6–12: Summary completion

Key

6   Sicilian (line 14)
7   grandfather (lines 28–29)
8   seventy (line 18)
9   over twenty countries (line 25)
10 three languages (line 160)
11 an interview (lines 151–153)
12 runs in families (line 146–147)

Questions 13–14: Multiple-answer question

Key

13–14 (in any order)
A. This reflects the text where it says *Language is known to be part of humans' unique cognitive endowment ... It is less clear, however, what upper limits this endowment has* (lines 38–44).

E. This also reflects the text in which the contributors agree that *an ability to learn many languages is the norm* (lines 101–102).
B. This is not stated in the text. C is also not the correct answer because although linguists suspect that hyperpolyglottism is passed on but do not know for sure, and they do not know how the process works. Similarly while some believe that hyperpolyglottism is the result of hard work others believe that the ability is not related to general intellectual ability, so D is also not correct.

Exploration

4 Key

a   described
b   claimed
c   disputed ... saying ... pointing out
d   doubts ... arguing
e   maintains

5 Possible answers

a   a   I'll tell you how my grandfather learned languages.
    b   Whatever port we visited, my grandfather knew the local language.
    c   I just don't believe the Mezzofanti story. I think it's absolutely preposterous, I mean, just think how long it would take anyone to learn seventy-two languages.
    d   I think it's very unlikely that anyone has the capacity to speak seventy-two languages. As far as I can see, it would take resources from other activities.
    e   I would say that exceptional language learners simply work harder.
b   a   N **insisted** that his grandfather ...
    b   N **stated** that whatever port ...
    c   A reader **challenged ... remarking** he found it preposterous, and **questioned** how long ...
    d   Philip Herdina **questioned** whether / **contending** that maintaining ...
    e   Stephen Krashen **insists** that exceptional ...

6 Possible answers

a   1   claimed / reported / found / shown
    2   conceded / admitted / confirmed
b   3   has claimed / has stated / has shown
    4   argue / maintain
c   5   suggests / believes / contends
    6   proposed / suggested / argued / insisted / maintained

7 Possible answers

a A willingness to try language out; not being worried about making mistakes; having an analytical mind; a good ear; ability to mimic; a good memory; a strong interest; a genuine motivation

d *Motherese* means the similar way in which mothers of all nationalities or language backgrounds talk to their babies. Whatever the actual language, mothers make the same noises to their very young babies (cooing, etc.).

e The main evidence is that 99% of humans use their own language correctly, applying grammar rules that they have not been taught.

Listening page 170

Issues – This section introduces the topic of the origins of language development.

Aims – Students practise sentence completion, multiple-answer and multiple-choice questions.

Orientation

1 Possible answers

a They are pre-programmed to absorb, process and reproduce the language used by the people around them.
Mothers are key because they have the closest contact with babies after they are born. Babies possibly know their mother's voice even before birth.

b Nonsense noises, cooing noises

c By using noises, as well as gestures and physical contact.

IELTS practice

Questions 1–5: Sentence completion

Key

1 repeat phrases
2 (kind of) framework
3 baby chimpanzee / chimp
4 pacify
5 words

Questions 6–9: Multiple-answer questions

Key

6, 7
A, C. The speaker says that early mothers probably made slings of some kind for ease of transportation and to keep their babies warm.

8, 9
A, C. The speaker says that *although the 'motherese' theory may account for the development of speech, it does not explain the development of grammar* (A). *Nor ... does it explain, how the sounds that mothers made acquired their meaning.* (C)

Question 10: Multiple-choice question

Key

10 C. The speaker talks about *recent research* and refers to *the new theory of motherese.*
A is false because although how mothers speak to their babies is mentioned in passing, this is not the speaker's main point. B is also mentioned in passing but is not the main point. The views of linguists and anthropologists D are mentioned, but this is not the main point, so D is also false.

Recording script

Emma: Hi, I'm Emma Bailey, and today I'm going to be talking 'baby-talk'. Hopefully, you'll find the subject interesting rather than infantile. I'd like to start by getting you to imagine a scenario. You're in an office or at a family gathering when a mother comes in with her young baby. Like everyone else, you want to see the mother and baby and you probably want to talk to the baby. How do you do this? What kind of language do you use? Recent research has shown that adults all talk to babies in similar ways: **they repeat phrases over and over again** in a high-pitched 'sing-song' voice with long vowel sounds. And if they ask questions they exaggerate their intonation. Researchers have discovered that this kind of language, which they have called 'motherese', is used by adults all over the world when they talk to babies. And according to a new theory, **'motherese' forms a kind of framework** for the development of language in children. This 'baby talk', so the theory goes, itself originated as a response to another aspect of human evolution: walking upright. In contrast to other primates, humans give birth to babies that are relatively undeveloped. So, whereas **a baby chimpanzee** can hold on to its four-legged mother and ride along on her back shortly after birth, helpless human babies have to be held and carried everywhere by their upright mothers. Having to hold on to an infant constantly would have made it more difficult for the mother to gather food. In this situation, researchers suggest, human mothers began putting their babies down beside them while gathering food. **To pacify an infant** distressed by this separation, the mother would 'talk' to her offspring and continue her search for food. This remote communication system could have marked the start of 'motherese'. As mothers increasingly relied on their voices to control the emotions of their babies, and, later, the actions of their mobile juveniles, **words emerged from the jumble of sounds and became conventionalized** across human communities, ultimately producing language.

Not all anthropologists, however, accept the assumption that early human mothers put their children down when they were looking for food. They point out that even modern parents do not do this. Instead, they prefer to hold their babies in their arms or carry them around in slings. They suggest that **early mothers probably made slings of some kind both for ease of transportation and to keep their babies warm** by holding them close to their bodies. If this was the case, they would not have needed to develop a way of comforting or controlling their babies from a distance. It is not only anthropologists, but also linguists who challenge this explanation for how language developed. They say that although the 'motherese' theory may account for the development of speech, **it does not explain the development of grammar. Nor**, they say, **does it explain, how the sounds that mothers made acquired their meaning**. Most experts believe that language is a relatively modern invention that appeared in the last 100,000 years or so. But if the latest theory is right, baby talk – and perhaps fully evolved language – was spoken much earlier than that. We know that humans were walking upright one and half million years ago. This means that mothers may have been putting their babies down at this time, and communicating with them in 'motherese'. We can be sure that this is not the end of the story, as anthropologists and linguists will continue to investigate the origins of this most human of abilities – language.

Exploration

2 Possible answers

a   Anthropologists study human behaviour and customs; linguists study the structure and development of languages. There is some overlap here, in so far as language is an aspect of human behaviour.

b   Anthropologists may be more likely than linguists to take a range of social and environmental factors into account when studying the development of human language, while linguists might look more at how languages change historically and geographically.

c   In many societies, the father's role is less significant than the mother's in the bringing up, and early education, of children. In general they would not have carried infants round with them while hunting or gathering.

Speaking page 171

Aims –   Students practise all sections of the IELTS Speaking Module.

IELTS practice
Part 1: Familiar discussion

1 Remind students that there are no right or wrong answers, and that they should give as full an answer as possible to each question, adding relevant examples where appropriate.

Part 2: Extended speaking

2 Remind students to keep their notes short and simple, and to speak clearly and not too slowly or too quickly.

3 Remind students to give a full answer with appropriate explanations or examples.

Part 3: Topic discussion

4 Remind students to give extended replies, by including reasons and adding more points connected with the topic to develop the discussion.

Language for writing page 173

Aims – Students revise features of sentence focus and emphasis which will be important for formal, academic writing.

Sentence focus

1 Possible answers

a, b i. These sentences begin by referring back to the previous sentence, and then add new information at the end.
ii. These sentences put the new information at the beginning.
Both sentences i are easier to understand because there is a clear connection between the two sentences.

2 Key

A competition took place recently to find the most popular words in the English language. The survey was carried out by The British Council. Suggestions were sent in by over 35,000 people. The most popular word, according to the results, was *mother*. Other words included in the top ten were *smile, love*, and *destiny*.

Placing emphasis

3 Key

b William Jones
c Many European and Asian languages are related.

4

a What can really help you gain confidence in your language ability is regular overseas travel.
b It was by adopting many words from other languages that English developed a huge vocabulary.
c It is for practical purposes such as business or study that most people learn English.
d It is the complex system of tones in Chinese that fascinates many people.
e It was in the late nineteenth century that the artificial language Esperanto was created.
f It is how the spelling rules of English work that most people have difficulty understanding. / What most people have difficulty understanding is how the spelling rules of English work.

5 Key

a It is by associating words with objects that children learn, according to one simple idea of language. What is not explained by this theory is how children learn prepositions or adjectives.
b Experiments have taken place to find out whether apes can learn simple languages. What they showed was some limited communication using signs and symbols.

Writing page 174

Issues – This section introduces the topic of the spread of English as a global language.
Aims – Students practise useful language for organizing, concession, cause and effect, and hypothesis.

Orientation

1 Key

a 300 million
b South America and the Caribbean: Guyana, Jamaica, Barbados, Trinidad and Tobago.
Africa: Botswana, Gambia, Ghana, Namibia, Uganda, Zambia, Zimbabwe. In Nigeria, Cameroon, and Swaziland, English shares official status.
Asia: Pakistan, India, Singapore, and the Phillipines.
Australasia: New Zealand, Australia, and Fiji.

Possible answers

c The use of English will almost certainly continue to increase because it is the language of computers and the Internet, and because it is the language of the world's most dominant culture (the USA).
d The spread of English is a threat to the cultural heritage of some countries, especially those where the mother tongue is in serious decline. Cultural expression which is largely language-based, such as novels and poetry, folk song and theatre, is liable to be swamped by English-language alternatives.

Useful language

2 Key

1 Firstly
2 Unless
3 As a result
4 On the other hand
5 Although
6 Furthermore
7 provided

3 Possible answers

Organizing: in the first place, secondly, moreover, finally, lastly, in conclusion
Concession: but, (and) yet, however, nevertheless, even though, despite, in spite of
Cause and effect: since, owing to, because of, consequently, therefore, as a result
Hypothesis: unless, provided, providing, if, otherwise

Think, plan, write

4 Key

a It should be compulsory for all children to study a second language as soon as they start school.

Help yourself page 176

The final page in each unit is intended to raise a variety of extra areas that students can explore and to encourage responsibility for their own language learning.

Pronunciation: word stress

2 Key

1 louder
2 longer
3 more

4 higher
5 bigger

4 Key

a <u>ea</u>sy
   <u>con</u>text
   <u>so</u>cial
   <u>lec</u>ture

b re<u>cord</u> (verb)   <u>rec</u>ord (noun)
   ob<u>ject</u> (verb)   <u>ob</u>ject (noun)
   ex<u>port</u> (verb)   <u>ex</u>port (noun)
   con<u>trast</u> (verb)   <u>con</u>trast (noun)

c com<u>pete</u>   compe<u>ti</u>tion
   <u>pho</u>tograph   pho<u>tog</u>raphy
   <u>ed</u>ucate   edu<u>ca</u>tion
   e<u>con</u>omy   eco<u>nom</u>ic
   <u>Chi</u>na   Chin<u>ese</u>
   <u>vol</u>untary   volun<u>teer</u>
   <u>ac</u>tive   ac<u>tiv</u>ity
   <u>lux</u>ury   lux<u>ur</u>ious

IELTS to do list

Encourage the students to tick one of the boxes and plan to do this task outside class.

Where to look

Students can use these practical tips to find further information.